Learning the R.O.P.E.S. For Improved Executive Function

A Cognitive Behavioral Approach for
Individuals with High Functioning Autism
and Other Behavioral Disorders

Patricia Schetter, M.A.

Autism and Behavior Training Associates

*"Helping you find the keys to
unlock the potential of students
on the Autism Spectrum"*

ABTA Publications
Redding, CA USA

Autism & Behavior Training Associates
ABTA Publications and Products
PO Box 492123
Redding, CA 96049

For information on ordering this manual or
on workshops provided by Autism & Behavior Training Associates on this and
other topics, please see our websites at:

www.autismandbehavior.com

www.abtaproducts.com

Learning the R.O.P.E.S. for Improved Executive Function

ISBN 978-0-9761517-0-8

Cover Design and photo by Mary A. Livingston

Printed in U.S.A.
Book manufacturing services provided by
Red Tail Custom Book Manufacturing
www.redtail.com

SUSTAINABLE   FIBER USED IN THIS PRODUCT SUPPLIED BY A PARTICIPATING
FORESTRY   MANUFACTURER AND MEETS THE SOURCING REQUIREMENTS
INITIATIVE   OF THE SFI PROGRAM. WWW.ABOUTSFI.ORG

FSC

Mixed Sources
Paper products from well-managed forests,
controlled sources and recycled wood or fiber
Cert. no. SW-COC-001592
www.sfc.org
©1996 Forest Stewardship Council

Dedicated to the extraordinary parents and educators working with these fascinating children and to the many children with high functioning autism who have allowed me to learn so much from them.

Table of Contents

Acknowledgements

There are so many people responsible for the completion of this manual. First and foremost, I must thank my husband John who endured many more tantrums and wet diapers than the average husband as he tended to our beautiful children while I squeezed in an hour or two of writing here and there. I thank my children, Owen and Andrew, for giving mommy the time to put these many strategies and experiences on paper. I surely would not have had this opportunity if I had not stepped away from the 40 hour work week to be with my boys. I also owe much gratitude and appreciation to my parents, Roger and Erma, who taught me so much about planning and the importance of thinking through all possible scenarios and outcomes. They also raised me to believe that anything is possible if you are persistent and if you keep your priorities in check.

The culmination of my experiences allowed me to write this book, however, a few people have had significant influence on my professional beliefs and understanding of this complex topic. I want to thank Joe Morrow and Brenda Terzich for introducing me to applied behavior analysis and working with this extraordinary population.

I must thank the White family for their trust and commitment and for teaching me so much about the issues faced by children and families affected by autism. I also owe much gratitude to Gail Cafferata, whose no nonsense approach to addressing behaviors and in depth knowledge of the classroom and public school system taught me about what works in school settings.

This acknowledgement would not be complete without mentioning my biggest cheerleaders and those who reviewed and provided technical support in the development of this manual. First, Lynne Weissmann, whose constant encouragement, support and feedback provided the motivation to keep this project going. Next, my reviewers, Victoria Bluett-Murphy, Gail Cafferata, Kandis Lighthall, Rodger Stein and Cathy Smith. I thank you all for your invaluable feedback and support. An extra note of thanks to Cathy Smith, for her technical and artistic expertise, and to her mother, Christie Wyman, for her professionalism in editing the manual.

Introduction

<u>About Executive Function and Autism</u>

"Executive Functions" are the cognitive processes thought to be responsible for many of our problem-solving skills and abilities. They are the planning processes that we automatically use at the beginning of a task and when dealing with novel situations. They are the "ability to maintain an appropriate problem solving set for the attainment of a future goal" (Welsh, M., and Pennington, S., 1988).

"Executive dysfunction" was originally identified in individuals who had sustained head injuries, typically in the frontal or prefrontal cortex. The common impairments in functioning for these individuals include: an inability to recall information, an inability to plan or organize information in a meaningful manner, an inability to maintain goal directed behavior, an inability to deal with novel situations, and, often, inflexible patterns of thinking. The correlation of symptoms between individuals with autism spectrum disorder (ASD) and those who have sustained frontal lobe injuries, and therefore impairments in executive function, was originally made in 1978 by Damasio and Maurer. Since that time there has been a plethora of research showing that deficits in executive functions are apparent in individuals with autism (for a review, see Pennington, S., and Ozonoff, S., 1996), with differences most often becoming apparent by age 5.5 (Dawson, G. and Lewy, A. 1998).

Ozonoff (2002) reported that individuals with ASD have certain executive functions that are impaired including; flexibility, organization and planning skills, and self-monitoring, while other executive function skills are spared, including inhibition such as, the conscious exclusion of unacceptable thoughts or desires.

In summary, the core executive dysfunctions or deficits in autism are:

- **R**ecalling and restating information in meaningful ways.
- **O**rganization and planning skills.
- **P**rioritizing and goal directed behavior.
- **E**valuating situations, actions and outcomes.
- **S**elf-management.

They need to learn the

R.O.P.E.S.

Behavior Problems Associated with Executive Dysfunction

Individuals often exhibit maladaptive patterns of behaviors that are a direct result of severe skill deficits. For example, a child who has deficits in his/her ability to communicate may engage in aggression, tantrums, or some other maladaptive behaviors to get what he/she needs or wants. The following are some of the common behavior problems associated with deficits in executive function:

Noncompliance: A child who is not able to recall the instruction given or who is unable to organize the steps he/she must follow to begin or complete a task is likely to appear "noncompliant." This is particularly true when he/she is able to restate the instruction but not begin the action. This is often the case for children on the autism spectrum. Teachers and parents may mistake the child's ability to restate the instruction for his/her true understanding of the process of the task. Simply because the child is able to repeat, "I need to get ready for math," he/she may not understand this includes: stopping reading the book, putting it away, getting out the math book, paper, and pencil, and looking at the board.

Prompt dependence: Children with executive dysfunctions often require and wait for extra cues or instructions to begin or complete tasks. For example, the teacher might say, "Get ready for math," and the student continues his previous action until the teacher approaches him, and gives a more direct instruction such as, "Put the reading book in your desk and take out your math book." This leads to a label of "prompt dependent." Often, while waiting for additional cues or instructions, they will engage in self-stimulating behavior such as humming, rocking, etc. or they will revert to other ritualized patterns of behavior such as repeating movie lines or perseverating on a favorite topic. These are called "off task behaviors" and often lead people to label these students "highly distractible." When self-management and goal directed behaviors are not taught, they may continue to be "prompt dependent" even on tasks they are capable of performing independently.

Disorganization: Many individuals with executive dysfunction appear very disorganized. Their desks, backpacks, or bedrooms may be in a constant state of disarray. They may have piles of "stuff" everywhere. They are accused of being packrats: never getting rid of anything, even things that appear to serve no functional purpose. These issues are primarily a result of the child's inability to sort, organize, and prioritize relevant materials. The child may also be attempting to compensate for deficits by using piles of "stuff" as a visual cue. For example, if a student leaves his/her math book out, he/she may see it and remember that he/she has math homework to complete.

Socially inappropriate behaviors: This includes saying or doing things that are seen as rude or uncaring. The child appears to have no empathy for others or to care about another person's perspective or feelings. For example, the student with high functioning autism may notice his teacher's new haircut and say, "Your hair looks strange." These behaviors are due to deficits in evaluation skills and self-management. The child is unable to objectively evaluate his/her own behavior and its potential outcomes to obtain the desired social outcome.

This inability to recognize the connection between behavior and its consequences, particularly the social consequences, often results in extreme difficulty with relationship development and maintenance.

They Don't Behave This Way On Purpose!

These behavior problems are associated with skill deficits. Individuals with executive dysfunction and high functioning autism have not successfully learned better ways to behave. Much like children who engage in tantrums because they are unable to communicate what they need, these children are engaging in maladaptive behaviors because they have not been effectively taught or sufficiently rewarded for doing things another, more acceptable way. A common misconception is they are capable of learning to behave differently; they are just lazy or unmotivated. Students with autism spectrum disorder and other neurological impairments, such as attention deficit disorder, obsessive compulsive disorder, etc. have differences in their brains that make them unable to learn things the way typical learners do (if they could, they would). They cannot learn a different way of behaving without specific targeted interventions. It is the responsibility of the parents and educators working with these children to address their specific deficits and find ways of teaching and reinforcing more appropriate and adaptive behaviors. *Learning the R.O.P.E.S. for Improved Executive Function* is an instructional manual designed for parents and educators to teach strategies to children with high functioning autism and other like disabilities, and provide them with the necessary structure and support to overcome the deficits associated with executive dysfunction. The approaches outlined in this manual are based on strategies for executive function retraining that have been effective with brain injured patients, the principles of applied behavior analysis, and many years of practical experience working with children with high functioning autism and other neuro-behavioral disorders.

Why This Manual Was Developed

Through my years of working with this population, I have seen core executive deficits interfere with my clients' abilities to achieve their highest potentials. Starting around the third grade, those children who have the intellectual capacity to be excellent students begin to fail due to their inability to plan, organize, and complete the increasingly complex assignments given in school. In addition, their inability to stay on track with the social, functional, and extra-curricular demands becomes overwhelming. As they fall behind and recognize their failures, many students with autism spectrum disorder become anxious and depressed. As a result of their frustration, many act out to protest the demands. Frequently, they are placed in highly restrictive settings, usually around students who are either much lower cognitively or who have severe emotional issues. The focus at that point is typically on decreasing all of their "maladaptive behaviors," but little is done to teach them the executive skills (recalling/restating information, organization, planning, prioritization and goal directed behavior, evaluation skills and self-management) that will eventually end their frustrations.

There are several resources for executive retraining in persons with traumatic brain injury, and much research has been done to support the effects of these strategies. There are currently no programs specifically designed to overcome executive skill deficits in children with autism. A search of the literature for methods to address these issues in students with autism reveals only bits and pieces of programs specifi-cally designed for this population. For example, the TEACCH program (www.teacch.com) provides many examples of how to use visual supports and structure to help children on the autism spectrum understand expectations and complete tasks more independently. Visual schedules, written/visual instructions, and work systems are very good methods for helping students with autism complete tasks and stay organized. But, these structures and supports, though effective, require an outside source to design, produce and manage. The student is typically not taught to set up and self-manage his/her own systems. In a comprehensive and functional executive skills training program, students must be trained to self-manage and self-advocate for the structures and supports they need to be successful.

These students have the capacity to learn many of these invaluable life skills. By utilizing cognitive and behaviorally based strategies and approaches that have been proven effective for teaching other skills to individuals on the autism spectrum, it is possible to teach executive skills. It is hoped that this manual will assist parents and educators in identifying and addressing these deficits early on, before frustration and behavior problems become the primary focus of intervention.

The Cognitive-Behavioral Approach

Many people are familiar with the behavioral approach in working with children on the autism spectrum. In this approach, there is a heavy emphasis on teaching overt behaviors through the use of various behavioral techniques, including task analysis, shaping, fading, prompting, and reinforcement. This approach is effective for increasing such skills as self-help, communication, play skills, and pre-academic skills. It is difficult when addressing issues such as executive functions to strictly use a behavioral approach since many of the skills we are trying to teach are "process" oriented rather than "product" oriented. In other words, we are more concerned with how the student reaches the conclusion about what to do than the actual act of doing it. In a cognitive-behavioral approach, the thinking process is the primary focus of the intervention; however, changes in overt behaviors are the desired outcome. In *Cognitive-Behavioral Therapy for Impulsive Children* (1993), Kendall and Brasswell show that there are several underlying principles in a cognitive-behavioral approach. The following is adapted from their work:

1. Cognitive processes are involved in human learning. Children develop these processes and representations as they gain experiences.

2. Thoughts, feelings and behavior are causally interrelated; therefore alterations to one element will have effects on the others. Thus, cognitive-behavioral approaches have a strong thinking-feeling-acting focus.

3. Cognitive activities, such as pre-event expectations, ongoing self-talk and post-event evaluation are important in understanding maladaptive behaviors and producing therapeutic change.

4. Cognitive processes can be cast into testable formulations that are integrated with behavioral approaches. It is desirable to combine cognitive treatment strategies with behavioral teaching approaches, such as shaping, fading, prompting and contingency management.

5. The goal of the cognitive-behavioral intervention is to identify maladaptive cognitive processes (ways of thinking), work with the child to remediate these thought processes, and show the behavioral changes and outcomes associated with these changes in thinking to the child so the changes will be maintained and generalized.

Cognitive-behavioral approaches have been shown to be effective in increasing problem solving and self-control (i.e., decreasing off task behaviors) in children with Attention Deficit Hyperactivity (ADHD) and Conduct Disorder (both involve executive dysfunction). For a review of these studies see Kendall and Braswell, (1993). Since research has demonstrated the effectiveness of a cognitive-behavioral approach in the treatment of maladaptive behaviors associated with executive dysfunction in these subgroups, it only makes sense to apply these techniques to children with high functioning autism who demonstrate similar patterns of behavior. In doing so, one must be sensitive to the distinct learning differences of children with autism. Their strengths in visual perception should be capitalized upon and their deficits in auditory processing should be recognized and adapted in the approach.

Who This Manual Is Intended For

This manual will assist parents, caregivers, and educators working with children with high functioning autism/Asperger's Syndrome, and similar behavioral disorders who are between the ages of eight years through adulthood. Although some suggestions for younger children are included, many of the skills targeted in this manual are not developmentally appropriate until around age eight or nine. In order to best prepare for the later development of executive skills, early learners should focus heavily on sorting and labeling based on multiple attributes, sequencing, prediction, recall, and following increasingly complex instructions (e.g., if/then), categorization, comparisons (e.g., same vs. different), and reasoning skills. These are all critical prerequisite skills.

Although instructions on how to teach the strategies in this manual are provided, details about specific behaviorally based techniques and how to implement them are not included. It is assumed that the reader has a fairly good understanding of basic behavioral teaching strategies, including the use of task analysis, shaping, fading, prompting, and reinforcement. In addition, although the use of positive behavior management plans is referred to in this manual, this manual is not intended to replace the development of such plans. These plans should be developed by qualified individuals trained in the field of applied behavior analysis and based on individual assessment; however, many of the strategies outlined in the manual can be used to teach alternative behaviors as part of a comprehensive behavior plan.

Using this Manual

In each of the upcoming chapters, I will discuss specific deficit areas. After a brief introduction, the chapter will provide an operational definition. To address each skill deficit associated with executive dysfunction, we must first operationally define the behaviors we will be teaching and measuring. An operational definition describes in very specific and concrete terms the behaviors or actions which are to be taught or displayed by the student. For a behavior to be operationally defined, it must be measurable so that any change in that behavior can be evaluated by objective data.

In summary, an operational definition must be:

- Specific
- Observable
- Measurable

Following the definition, specific types of interventions will be covered to address the identified deficit. These include the following types of interventions:

- Strategies: Specific behaviors and skills that are taught to help the person overcome or compensate for his/her deficits.

- Structure: Modifications to the environment or routines that will better accommodate the needs of the learner.

- Supports: Assistance from others or specific devices that will help facilitate independence.

In the text and the appendices that follow, specific models and worksheets are provided. Many of the worksheets are in graphic organizer formats. The graphic organizer is "a visual representation of knowledge" (Bromley, K., Irwin-DeVitas, L., and Modlo, M., 1995). Graphic organizers facilitate learning by helping students organize ideas and see relationships between different pieces of information. Research has shown that "creating and using graphic organizers to illustrate the organization of ideas and information aids comprehension and learning" (Flood, J., and Lapp, D., 1988; Heimlich, J., and Pittelman, S., 1986). Graphic organizers have been shown to be effective with a wide variety of learners, including those with learning disabilities and high functioning autism. The aim is to "provide the learner with a system that is easy to use but that they will find useful and valuable in many ways for the rest of their lives" (Pehrsson, R., and Denner, P., 1989). Although the typical use of graphic organizers is to address specific academic tasks, we will be utilizing them in a very different way to address cognitive and problem solving processes across all domains.

The types of graphic organizers used in this book are:

Cluster Organizers: This type of organizer states knowledge and shows how parts pertain to a whole. It is good to use when integrating new knowledge with previously learned material and when "brainstorming" a topic or idea. It is also useful when attempting to break down specific skills or topics into component parts. Using this type of graphic organizer is often called "webbing."

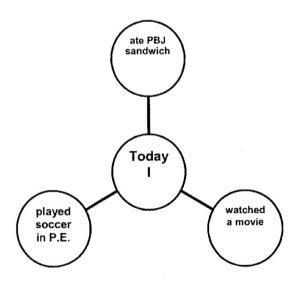

Sequential Organizers: These organizers depict action sequences. They demonstrate the order or progression of a particular act or situation. They are very useful for prioritizing or putting parts in a logical order for a particular desired outcome.

Venn Diagram: This type of organizer is often used to show relationships between sets. It is useful for examining similarities and differences and it is frequently used as a pre-writing activity to enable students to organize thoughts prior to writing a compare/contrast essay.

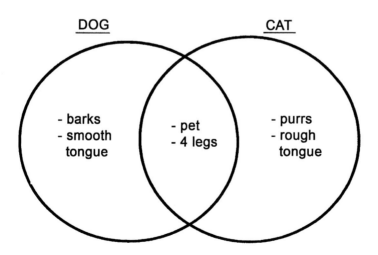

Chapter 1

Recalling and Restating

Understanding Deficits in Recalling and Restating
In Individuals with High Functioning Autism

The ability to recall information that was previously presented and reproduce past actions, in a sense, is the outcome of learning. In our current standards-based educational system, memorizing and restating facts is the product and measurable way we determine if a student learned and knows the information we intended to teach. For example, we test students on their ability to recall facts and information. If they are successful at recalling the information, we say that they have learned it. As a result, they generally get good grades and are considered to be "good students."

Students on the autism spectrum, particularly those who score high in intelligence, are often very successful when it comes to memorizing facts and performing tasks that require procedural recall. For example, they are usually good at spelling, decoding, and computation in math. Because of these strengths, they often get good grades in these subject areas and in the early elementary grades where procedural skills are primarily taught. They have a very difficult time, however, remembering and reproducing tasks and information which require declarative recall (i.e., recalling knowledge about things and relationships between things). Examples of skills requiring this type of recall include reading comprehension, solving word problems, predicting or making inferences, and conceptual understanding. Due to these deficits, students on the autism spectrum tend to struggle in subjects that require this type of recall and reasoning. In elementary school, there is typically a shift at around third grade to tasks and subject matter that require these skills (e.g., creative writing, book reports and the like). This is often when we begin to see very bright children on the autism spectrum start to fall behind and become increasingly frustrated with learning, homework, and school in general.

Although students with high functioning autism are often very good at rote memorization of information and facts, they do not integrate the information with previously learned facts (i.e., their memories are not effectively organized) to truly develop an understanding of concepts. For example, the typical child will learn a foundational piece of information such as "this is a dog," and then integrate new information as he/she is exposed to it (e.g., dogs are different colors, sizes, and breeds, but they are all dogs). Eventually the idea of a dog becomes fairly well integrated and he/she has the "concept" of what a dog is. Then, as the child is exposed to new concepts such as "animals," he/she integrates the previous knowledge (previously learned information about dogs, cats, horses, cows, etc.) with the new information, and new concepts or categories are formed. Typical learners are able to organize and integrate information and see relationships as new information is learned. They recognize the similarities and differences between old information and new, and then organize the information in their memories for later use or recall.

Children with high functioning autism learn new facts but do not integrate the information well with previously learned facts. They lack the ability to effectively organize the information in their memories and to see the "whole picture." This has been described as a lack of central coherence by Uta Frith and her colleagues. Frith (1989) describes central coherence as "the ability to draw together diverse information to construct higher level meaning in context." In typical learners, there is a tendency to form concepts and make sense of fragmented information based on previous knowledge and current context. Individuals with high functioning autism do not do this. Instead, information is compartmentalized, rather than assimilated. This is illustrated by the writings of Temple Grandin, an adult woman with autism. In her book, Thinking In Pictures, she says, "...each new piece of information is in its own separate file. Being autistic, I don't naturally assimilate information that most people take for granted. Instead, I store information in my head as if it were on a CD-ROM disc" (Grandin, T.,1995).

Due to these differences in how people take in new information and their inability to effectively organize it, we must use explicit structures to help organize the information for them if we expect them to truly learn and recall concepts. In addition, they must learn strategies for organizing, integrating, and recalling information independently so they will not need to rely on others to provide accommodations for the rest of their lives.

Research has shown that recall is facilitated greatly if the information is well organized at the time of learning (Pehrsson, R., and Denner, P., 1989). Therefore, these skill deficits (i.e., recall and organizational skills) cannot really be thought of as mutually exclusive. Students rely on their abilities to successfully organize information at "input" in order to successfully recall and integrate the information later as "output." Most individuals with autism do not organize incoming information in a functional manner for later use, particularly when the incoming information is auditory. It has been well documented that visual perceptual skills and visual memory skills are areas of strength for most people on the autism spectrum. We also know based on many autobiographical accounts, such as Temple Grandin's, that auditory information is very confusing and hard for people with autism to attend to, organize, and interpret.

These deficits in organization and recall have profound impacts on social skills and conversational skills. Many individuals with autism are not even able to organize personal experiences in their memories and relate these experiences to others. The prime example is the student who cannot tell you what he/she did five minutes after he/she did it. Surely the child has not forgotten what he/she just did, he/she is simply unable to organize the information in his/her memory, put it in sequence, and relay the information in a meaningful way. Many people with high functioning autism feel they are better able to express their thoughts and personal experiences in writing, or typing/drawing if motor skills are impaired. This is a much less dynamic process than speaking. They are able to see, visually, the representations of their thoughts and reorganize them as needed.

Deficits in recall also impair school functioning when it comes to the ability to recall and complete assignments. Because students with high functioning autism have such poor organization and recall abilities, they will often forget to take home the assignments and materials, or fail to complete or turn in important assignments. As a result, their grades suffer. Many times the student will complete the necessary assignments for a class but simply forget to turn them in. Or, they are unable to find the completed work when it comes time to turn it in because it is lost in the abyss called the backpack. The effort was put forth to complete the work, but due to deficits in recall and organization, the product was never given to the teacher for a grade. Strategies for teaching students to keep track of assignments and the materials needed to complete the assignments, as well as structural supports which facilitate completion of work, are critical elements of an educational plan for students with high functioning autism and executive dysfunction.

In addition to using recall and memory skills and abilities in academic tasks and settings, we rely heavily on these skills to perform functional living routines. When we are young, we learn simple self-help tasks like dressing and brushing our teeth. It is our increasing motor control and our procedural memory of how to complete the steps of these tasks that allows us to become independent. As we grow, we learn more complex routines such as a "bedtime routine" in which we recall and perform many related tasks in a sequential order. Usually we complete these routines without even thinking of the steps we are completing. We go on "auto pilot." We are even able to multi-task while completing these routines, easily shifting our attention back and forth from one thing to the other. For example, we can easily talk on the phone while pouring a cup of coffee. Individuals on the autism spectrum are not able to handle interruptions in their learned procedures or deal with changes. While they may know how to procedurally complete a functional living routine such as dressing, they often have a very difficult time doing it independently.

Many parents of children on the autism spectrum begin expressing extreme concern about their child's hygiene skills around seventh grade. The parents may indicate that the child "does not seem to care if he has dirty teeth, bad breath, and body odor." Poor hygiene will often have social implications; other kids may begin teasing or isolating the child with high functioning autism because of his poor hygiene. The idea that these hygiene deficits are primarily due to a lack of motivation (the student with autism just does not care about the social implications) is an incomplete analysis, and to address only the social aspects of hygiene will not solve the problem. Hygiene and self-care issues have much more to do with deficits in planning and the shifting attention required for completing these complex self-care routines. It is very important when addressing these types of issues that we recognize and accommodate these learning differences by utilizing the necessary structures and supports to allow maximum independence.

Due to visual strengths, the use of visual strategies must be capitalized on when addressing issues of recall and organization. We must utilize visual organizational strategies when presenting information to students on the autism spectrum if we expect them to develop concepts and integrate new information into their memories. Graphic organizers are one method for accommodating this learning difference. By utilizing them, we are essentially showing the child with autism how to effectively organize the necessary information in his/her memory for later functional use.

In this chapter, you will learn how to use graphic organizers, specifically the cluster type organizers, to help children with high functioning autism better recall and organize information so it can be integrated with other knowledge for functional use. You will also learn how to use visual structures and supports to capitalize on this area of strength in an attempt to promote more independent functioning.

The Operational Definition of Recalling and Restating

The ability to restate information (including verbal instructions, text, and personal experiences), follow multi-step directions, and complete multi-step tasks, without requiring additional prompting from another person.

Recalling/Restating: Strategies

Strategies are those behaviors and skills that are taught to help a person overcome or compensate for skills deficits. In the following section some strategies for helping individuals with high functioning autism overcome and/or compensate for executive deficits in recalling and restating will be discussed.

Graphic Organizers

Using Graphic Organizers to Facilitate Recall of Personal Experiences and Events

This case example illustrates a concern often expressed by teachers and parents: the child's inability to recall and relate personal experiences in a coherent manner.

Graphic organizers can be used to assist the child in recalling and organizing information about his/her day, or other personal experiences so he/she can later discuss them in conversations with others (refer to the completed example in Figure 1).

Case Example

Tanner's mom was extremely concerned about his inability to tell her about his day when he would arrive home from school. He was even unable to tell his mother about activities he had completed 5 minutes earlier. He was a very bright boy with an above average IQ. He had the language to describe the activities, yet he would not do it without significant prompting and probing by his mother. This deficit was very upsetting to Tanner's mother and significantly impacted his ability to take part in conversations with his family.

Graphic Organizer for
Recalling Personal Experiences

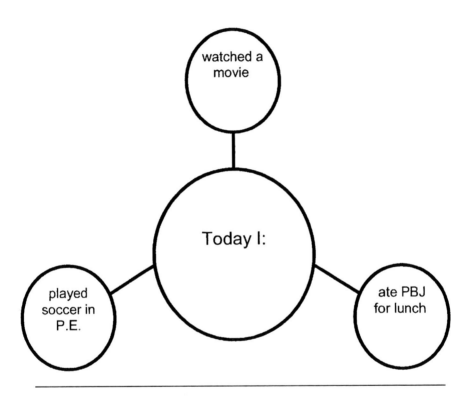

Figure 1. Example of how a graphic organizer was used to assist Tanner with recalling the events of his day. Initially his Mother wrote the information in the graphic organizer after asking him fairly specific questions, such as, "What did you eat?" Eventually Tanner was able to recall fairly specific events and fill in the organizer independently.

Teaching this Strategy

- To effectively begin using the graphic organizer to facilitate recall of events, first show the student the organizer and explain that it is a tool used to help people remember and organize information.

- It may be more interesting to the student to introduce the organizer immediately following the completion of several highly preferred activities. This may need to be intentionally set up just prior to the initial teaching session for this new skill. For example, the speech therapist could set up a "free choice day" and allow the student to select three highly preferred activities. Immediately following the completion of these activities, introduce the graphic organizer activity for recalling events.

- Start by filling in the topic in the middle bubble and then ask the child to verbally provide information about his/her day or a specific personal experience. The teacher/parent will initially write the information in a bubble as it is provided. Later, the student will be required to fill in the bubbles while the teacher/parent provides only positive and/or corrective feedback.

- If the child is unable to provide information, the questions should become more specific. For example, start by asking, "Can you tell me one thing you did today?" If the student provides an answer, the information is written into a bubble. If the student is unable to answer the general question, ask a more specific question like, "What did you eat today?" or, "Who did you see today," etc.

- Start small, only requiring two to three pieces of informa-tion to complete the organizer.

- Initially, reinforce any attempt at an answer. As the student becomes more proficient, make sure that the answers are factual (i.e., make sure the student is not just perseverating on a favorite topic and stating that he/she did something that he/she did not actually do). It may be necessary to have a list of the day's activities available to check the validity of the student's response.

- As the student becomes better at recalling events, the organizer can be expanded to five bubbles, seven bubbles, and so on. In addition, the use of the organizer needs to be transferred to the student, so he/she should begin writing in the answers and filling out the organizer in its entirety prior to receiving feedback. This will be dis-cussed further in Chapter 5, Self-Management.

- If the student is unable to come up with any information at all, it will be necessary to have a very specific log of daily activities so that the teacher/parent can ask a "choice of two" question. For example, "did you eat peanut-butter and jelly (the correct answer) or tuna fish (the incorrect answer) for lunch?"

Bright Idea

If the student is not successful at recalling events even when the "choice of two" prompt is used, it may be necessary to go back to a more concrete and visual process. To do this, you will need photos of him/her engaging in daily activities. Or remnants of the day's activities. NOTE: These are also very good skills to work on with early learners (pre-k through age 8).

- The student is taught how to sort the pictures into piles ("things I did today" and "things I did not do today").

- Once he/she knows how to sort, teach him/her to answer the question, "What did you do today?" while the pictures (things he/she did and distracters or things he/she did not do), are on the table in front of him/her.

- When he/she is able to answer the question accurately, approximately 80 percent of the time, reintroduce the graphic organizer.

- Use the photos to prompt the verbal answers that will be written into the graphic organizer. To do this, show the student the picture while asking the question, "What did you do today." Systematically, a time delay should be added between the question and the presentation of the prompt (the photo). The student should be given a more highly desired reward for an anticipated response (i.e., before the picture is shown), and a lower level of reinforcement for a prompted response (i.e., he responds only when shown the picture).

- The pictures should be systematically faded as the student is able to provide answers without seeing the pictures first (i.e., he/she is consistently "beating the prompt").

Using Graphic Organizers to Recall Instructions and Break Tasks Down

Often the child with autism is unable to recall a set of instructions given, or he/she can restate the instructions but is not able to break the instructions down into simple doable tasks. A cluster type organizer can be used to facilitate recall of instructions and to further break the instructions down into succinct tasks (see example in Figure 2).

Case Example

Nathaniel's mom was very frustrated with his "non-compliance." She would give him a set of instructions or chores and he would not complete them. She would even have him repeat the instructions to her after she gave them, which he could do with no problem, yet he would not do the chores without her constantly nagging him and eventually walking him through the tasks step by step. She finally tried taking away his most prized possession (Nintendo), but to no avail. This consequence only resulted in extreme melt-downs, but no increase in compliance. Finally, she recognized that he was not being "noncompliant" at all, but that there was some other underlying deficit standing in the way of his completing these tasks. Once she made this mind shift, she was able to address the problem effectively.

Graphic Organizer for
Recalling and Breaking Down Instructions

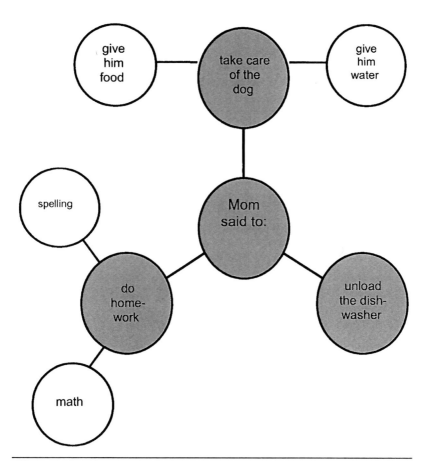

Figure 2. Example of how a cluster organizer was used to help Nathaniel remember a set of instructions and break the instructions down into manageable tasks. The shaded bubbles are the initial set of instructions. The white bubbles are breakdowns of the instructions into more specific and manageable tasks/steps.

Teaching this Strategy

- Use of the graphic organizer for this purpose is taught in the same way as described above. The student should first be shown the organizer (shaded sections only) and told that it is a tool to be used to assist with remembering instructions and breaking tasks down.

- Begin by filling in the center bubble. This is the general instruction or content area to be recalled or broken down.

- Next, have the student recall the set of instructions. Start by giving very general verbal cues as needed such as, "What did Mom say to do?" and work to more specific verbal cues if needed, such as, "Were there any chores you needed to remember?" or even more specific, "Do you need to do something with the dishes?" Make sure to reinforce answers or attempts at answers initially.

- If necessary, use the "choice of two" questioning de- scribed above. For example, you might ask the child, "Do you need to load or unload the dishes?"

- Once the recall portion (shaded portion in Figure 2) is completed, the next step is to teach the student to break down each task. This is taught in the same manner.

- For this piece of the organizer, it is necessary to draw in the bubbles as needed. Start with the simplest skill (the one with the fewest sub-skills) and work to the more complex (the one with the most sub-skills).

- Draw a bubble with a line (as shown in Figure 2) and ask the student to state one step in the component. For example, "What is one step involved in taking care of the dog?" When the student answers, fill in the bubble. Reward attempts and correct responses.

- Order does not matter at this point. For example, the student does not need to come up with "first I should get her some water" as the initial step even though that may logically be the first thing to do. Sequencing the steps and putting them in a logical order will be addressed in Chapter 2, Organization and Planning Skills.

- Additional bubbles should be added and the process repeated. Use more specific questions and prompts as necessary. In this example, the teacher/parent could have the student look at the empty dog dishes when determining the steps, if needed. This would provide a very concrete visual cue.

- The goal of this procedure is for the student to become independently able to recall instructions, and begin to break more complex instructions down. He/she may become independent at completing the graphic organizer, or may even begin to "think through" the process. Regardless of the method acquired, the student will become less reliant on others and feel more competent and in control once a process for breaking down complete tasks/instructions is acquired.

Bright Idea

If the student is not successful at breaking down skills using the graphic organizer, it may be necessary to go back to a more concrete and visual process.

To do this, the teacher/parent will need photos of the student engaging in all of the steps of specific activities.

NOTE: These are also very good skills to work on with early learners (pre-k through age 8).

- Give the student a pile of pictures containing all of the steps of a designated task and some "distracters" (photos of him/her doing steps from another task).

- Have the student sort or otherwise identify which pictures are steps of the stated tasks. For example, photos of the student doing the steps for cleaning his/her room are put in a pile with pictures of the student doing unrelated tasks. The student is asked to sort or pick out all of the pictures that are steps for cleaning his/her room.

- Once the student is successfully identifying steps of various tasks in this manner, try using the photos as prompts with the cluster organizer.

- To do this, re-present the organizer and show the student one of the pictures while asking, "What are the steps of cleaning your room?"

- Systematically, a time delay should be added between the question and the presentation of the prompt (the photo). The student should be given a more highly desired reward for an anticipated response (i.e., before the picture is shown), and a lower level of reinforcement for a prompted response (i.e., he/she responds only when shown the picture).

- The pictures should be systematically faded as the student is able to provide answers without seeing the pictures first (i.e., he/she is consistently "beating the prompt")

Using Graphic Organizers to Facilitate Recall from Lectures and Written Material

Case Example

Alan's teacher, Mrs. Gunther, could not understand why he was doing so poorly in science and social studies. He was very smart and was at the top of his class in spelling and math. She knew that he could read faster than anyone in the class and that he regularly completed his reading assignments during class time in order to avoid having to take them home as homework. So why was he not able to answer any of the test questions or participate in class discussions when he was called on?

Alan's is a common story among students with high functioning autism. They listen to the lectures and discussions, but are unable to extract any meaningful information from them. For Alan, we began having him fill in a cluster organizer after listening to a lecture or reading the text to facilitate recall of important information (refer to Figure 3). Some students may be able to fill out the organizer while listening to the lecture (or while reading a text), but this shifting of attention (from listening/reading to writing) could be very difficult for some other students on the autism spectrum. It might be better to start by having these students listen to a segment of the lecture (or read a section of the text) and then immediately fill in the organizer by recalling important information from that section. Breaking the text or lecture up into smaller segments will help while the student learns this process. his can be done as a teacher lead whole class activity. The teacher can model the process on an overhead while the students fill in their graphic organizer.

Graphic Organizer for Recalling Information from Lecture or Text

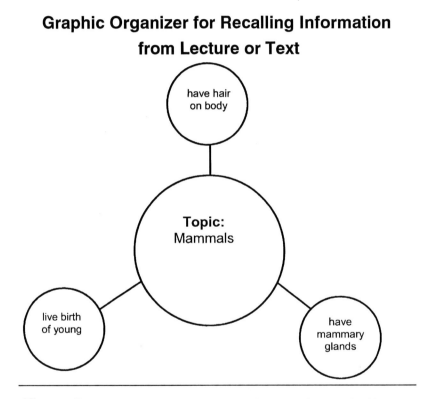

Figure 3. Example of a graphic organizer used to assist Alan with recalling important information from a class lecture. Alan listened to a lecture on mammals. During the lecture, he used the graphic organizer to record three important or key points about mammals from the lecture. Allen was then able to answer the comprehension questions related to mammals on the quiz as he had an effective visual way to organize and recall the information.

Graphic Organizer for Recalling Information from Lecture or Text (with additional prompts)

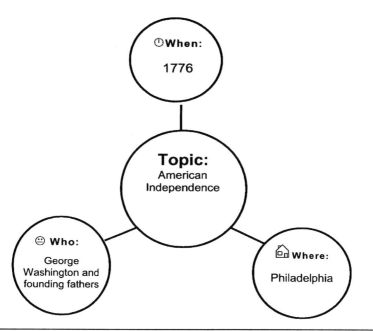

Figure 4. This is an example of how additional visual cues can be added to assist the student with discriminating which pieces of information are most relevant in the text or lecture. The bubble with the clock cues the student to recall when the events occurred, the stick figure designates the important people, the house cues recall of the location or place.

Teaching this Strategy

- Begin by explaining to the student that the organizer is a tool that can be used to help with note taking and studying.

- The center bubble should be filled in with the topic. This should initially be done by the teacher, but should be transferred to the student when he/she becomes more proficient at using the organizer for this purpose.

- Initially, ask the student to recall only one important piece of information about the topic. When the student provides the information, show the student how to write it in a bubble to complete the organizer. The student should be rewarded for each correct response and for attempts.

- If prompting is required, reread/restate the section of the text or lecture. Pause after a key point is made. Immediately, ask the student to identify the key point. Systematically add time delays between the repeat prompt and the pause/question.

- Shaping should be used to systematically increase the number of key points the student is expected to recall. Each important point or key piece of information the student recalls should be added in its own bubble to the graphic organizer.

- Eventually a reward should be provided only after the student completes the entire organizer independently, identifying eighty percent or more of the key points from the reading or lecture.

- If the student is unable to distinguish between important versus less relevant information, additional visual prompts can be taught and added to the organizer to assist the student with identifying which pieces of information are important (refer to Figure 4).

- If using an overhead projector, this is an excellent whole class strategy to teach effective note taking. Provide each student in class with a blank graphic organizer to fill in as the whole group goes through the process.

Bright Idea
Another method for teaching discrimination of important versus less relevant information is a simple sorting task.

- Sentences, phrases, or key words from the lecture or text are written on 3 x 5 cards.
- The student is asked to sort the cards into piles (one pile is important information, the other is less relevant). Initially the teacher should make the discrimination very easy. For example, important information about mammals are: they have mammary glands, are warm blooded, have body hair. Less relevant information is: mammal starts with M and ends with L, mammal is a six letter word. Once these easy discriminations are mastered, make the discriminations increasingly difficult. For example, "a cow is a mammal" is less relevant than "all mammals have mammary glands."
- When the student is able to sort important versus less relevant, he/she should then be taught how to put the information in a sequence from most important to least important. This is a critical skill to work on. It will prepare him/her for prioritization, which will be discussed further in Chapter 3.
- The eventual outcome of these strategies is for the student to be able to recall and restate key pieces of information from written and verbal sources without requiring additional prompts from another person. The student may be able to do this by filling in a graphic organizer before restating the information or may "think through" the process prior to restating the information. Either is acceptable.

Using Graphic Organizers as a Study Tool

The graphic organizer can be used as a study tool to assist the student in remembering important information about topics upon which he/she will later be tested. This is done by having the student practice reproducing the information from the graphic organizer (e.g., the one from the class lecture on mammals) onto a blank page. The graphic organizer will provide a visually organized method for remembering the important information about the topic. The student will be able to rely on this "map" when it is time for a test on the information. He/she will also be able to use this "map" to integrate new information later. This was a highly effective strategy for Alan. He went from receiving D's and F's to earning A's and B's in a matter of weeks.

Teaching this Strategy

- Begin by having the student review the original written organizer notes for a couple of minutes. This is likely the organizer that he/she completed during the class lecture or while reading a chapter from the text.

- Next provide a blank page and ask the student to reproduce the information as it was on the original organizer. Ask "What can you remember about _____ topic?"

- Allow the student to use the original organizer as a prompt if he/she has trouble recalling the information.

- Once the student is able to reproduce the complete organizer without accessing the prompt, the information is "learned" and he/she should be able to successfully retrieve the knowledge at a later date.

- Once the information is retained, practice asking specific "wh" questions. Have the student refer back to his notes if necessary to assist with answering the questions.

- The goal for this procedure is for the student to retain the information in his/her (visual) memory in order to successfully answer specific comprehension questions. This process is not going to insure that the student will utilize the information to integrate new knowledge. Have the student keep the graphic organizers in the appropriate school binder just as other students keep their notes. He/she will need to refer back to his/her "visual notes" to study as new information is acquired and assimilated (this is covered in the next section).

Using Graphic Organizers to Integrate New Information and Ideas

Once the student is reliably able to reproduce graphic organizers which represent previously learned information and ideas, we want him/her to utilize this to integrate new information as it is acquired (refer to Figure 5).

Graphic Organizer for Integrating New Information

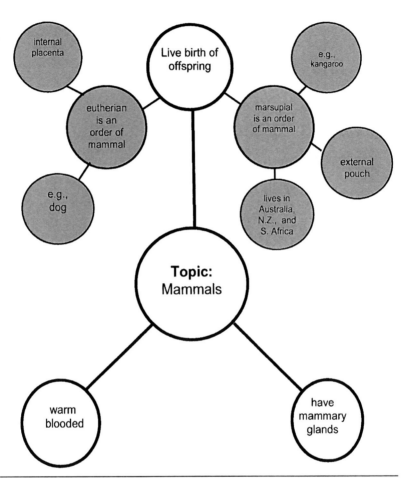

Figure 5. In this example, the new knowledge about marsupials and eutherians was integrated with the old knowledge of mammals. The shaded bubbles represent the new knowledge being integrated. The white bubbles represent the prior knowledge or the foundational information. You will see in the coming chapters how to expand on these basic uses of graphic organizers for recall to assist the student in the organization and planning process necessary for task completion.

Teaching this Strategy

- To teach this integration skill, ask the student to reproduce from memory an organizer about a specific topic. The student may not remember all of the elements of the original organizer. Reward him/her for what he/she does recall and refer him/her back to the "visual notes" to acquire the other information.

- After he/she has successfully reproduced the organizer, have him/her set it aside while the new related information is provided and reviewed, either in lecture or written format.

- After the student has heard or read the new information, ask him/her to integrate it into the old organizer. The teacher may need to add some visual structure at first (the arms and bubbles) so the student sees where the information should be integrated. Once he/she can add the new information, then he/she should actually write in the needed arms and bubbles in the correct places. This can be done through modeling and through prompting and corrective feedback.

- Remember that the student may need to continue to recreate the written graphic organizer to facilitate "thinking through the process." This is okay. Many students are eventually able to think through the process without writing it down.

The point of teaching visual note taking is to teach a "process". The student's ability to use the information at the appropriate time will require planned, explicit instruction and many opportunities for practice. The desired outcome or "product" is that the student is able to perform well on the tests and assignments given and ultimately succeed in life tasks and career. This will take some time, but with persistence the student can learn this new way of thinking.

Alarms and Timers

The use of timers and alarms are strategies we all use to aid us with recall. The timer on our oven reminds us to check what we are cooking; the alarm on our dryer reminds us to see if our clothes are dry; the timer on the treadmill counts down the number of minutes remaining. We even have alarms on our desktops that remind us when it is time for a specific appointment or meeting. For individuals with high functioning autism, using alarms and timers can be incorporated in many ways to aid in recall.

There are a variety of products now available on the market for this specific purpose. The WatchMinder (www.watchminder.com) is one example specifically made for individuals with attention deficit disorder and other learning disabilities (refer to Figure 6). It is a programmable watch that signals with various auditory cues when the person should do specific things. For example, the WatchMinder might chime at 12:00 noon and the display would read "Meds." It might signal at 2:00 p.m. and display, "Go to _____." It also has functions specifically for increasing self-management skills; including self-administering reinforcers (refer to Chapter 5).

I also like the Time Timer (www.timetimer.com). This is a visual timer that counts down and shows how much time is remaining with numbers and a strip of red. (refer to Figure 7). When the red is gone and the timer arm reaches 0:00, the time is up. This is very helpful for visual learners as a quick reference and for younger children who may not yet understand the concept of time. Time Timer is also an excellent tool for teaching self-management as discussed in Chapter 5.

Figure 6. The WatchMinder (www.watchminder.com) works very well for assisting students with beginning and finishing open ended tasks.

Figure 7. The Timetimer (www.timetimer.com) is another excellent tool for teaching students to start and stop open ended activities.

Using Timers in Open Ended Tasks

Case Example

Kimmy was a "Mommy's helper" and loved to help with the gardening and cooking. One day Kimmy asked if she could help her parents in the yard as they were preparing their summer garden. They said "sure" and told her to go to the backyard and water the beds so they could plant them next. Kimmy went to the backyard excited about helping. While Mom and Dad were busy in the front yard, Kimmy watered the beds. About 30 minutes later, Kimmy's Mom finally realized she had not yet returned. Thinking that perhaps Kimmy got side tracked playing with her toys, she proceeded with the gardening. About 30 minutes after that, Kimmy's Dad went to the back of the house to get fertilizer from the shed, only to find Kimmy there standing in a huge puddle of mud still watering the beds. He asked her why she did not stop. She said, "I did not know when I was done."

Timers can help remind a person when to stop an open ended activity. Often it is difficult for people with autism to shift their attention from one activity to another, particularly when they are engaging in an activity that does not have automatic closure. It is fairly clear when to stop unloading the dishwasher, when all the dishes are put away, but when should one stop watering the planting beds? The use of timers can aid students with high functioning autism in remembering to stop the activity after a preset amount of time. For example, a timer could have helped Kimmy know when to stop watering. Timers can also indicate when to stop open ended assignments such as reading or studying.

It is important when setting time limits to base them on several factors. First, you must find out how much time is available for the activity (this will be discussed in the coming chapters). Next, you must know the person's tolerance for a certain task. If he/she is only able to sit still for 10 minutes at a time, you will know not to set the time limit for more than about 8 minutes. If you are using the timer to indicate the end of a break, you should predetermine how long the break needs to be for the person to be physically and emotionally ready to go back to the task at hand. Once you have established these general parameters, you are ready to teach the student to use the timer for open ended tasks.

Teaching this Strategy

- The student should check the schedule to determine what the next activity is. The teacher or parent should then show the student the timer and explain that the timer will indicate when it is time to end that activity and move on to the next.

- Set the timer for the predetermined amount of time and remind the student that when the timer expires (as indicated by the auditory cue, or in the case of the Time Timer, when the red is gone) the student will need to stop what he/she is doing, check the schedule, and move on to the next activity. It can be helpful to write the next activity on a cue card and place it directly on the timer.

- Although initially an instructor will be setting the timer, the student will eventually be responsible for this step.

- Once the timer has expired, see if the student remembers what to do. If he/she successfully stops the current activity and moves onto the next, provide the student with reinforcement.

- If the student stops the activity, but does not move onto the next one, use an indirect verbal cue such as, "What should you do now that _____ is finished?" If he/she still does not know, provide a more direct verbal cue such as, "Where do you need to look to find the answer?" If he/she still does not respond, give a directive such as, "Check your schedule," or simply point to the schedule.

- If the timer expires and the student does not stop the initial activity, approach the student with the timer and provide an indirect prompt such as tapping the timer and giving an expectant look. If he stops and then transitions, provide reinforcement.

- If needed, provide increasingly direct cues such as, "Look, the time has expired, what does that mean?" "What do you need to do now?" If necessary, review the timer procedure completely with the student and then give a direct instruction to stop the activity and go on to the next.

- The eventual goal is for the student to independently set the timer, do the task, stop the task once the time has expired, move on to the next activity as indicated without requiring additional prompts or cues from another person. This is a process and will take time for the student to learn.

Using Timers to Limit Activities

Limiting highly preferred activities and interests is yet another difficult thing for individuals with high functioning autism. Many people try to prevent kids with autism from engaging in their "obsessions" or areas of interest, or they attempt to decrease these behaviors through the use of punishment. A far better strategy is to allow the activities under certain conditions and for only a preset amount of time. A timer is a necessity when working on this type of program. It can be used to remind the individual how long it is until he/she is allowed the highly preferred activity. It can also be used to remind him/her how much time is left to enjoy the highly preferred activity. These strategies will be discussed further in Chapter 5, in procedures for teaching self-management of behaviors.

Checklists

Using Task and Routine Checklists

In this strategy, a written or visual list is provided with step-by-step instructions for a specific task or routine. This is a strategy for teaching these students to compensate for problems with shifting attention and working memory. The student is first taught how to use the checklist: crossing off or checking off the steps as they are completed. Once he/she is successfully using the checklists, he/she should be taught how to write them. To accomplish this, he/she will also need to work on organization and planning skills (discussed in the next chapter) to determine the steps and material needed to complete a task. Refer to Figures 8 and 9 for examples of checklists for daily routines in the home and school settings.

Night-time Routine Checklist

DONE

Take off clothes ☐

Put in hamper ☐

Shower ☐

Get night time routine box ☐

Brush teeth ☐

Put on P.J.s ☐

Set alarm clock ☐

Reviewed By: ☐

Figure 8. Example of a checklist for a daily routine in the home setting

Ready To Go Home Routine Checklist

DONE

Take out Homework Summary Page ☐

Get all needed materials ☐

Put materials in backpack ☐

Put Homework Summary Page in backpack ☐

Collect all items in "Out Box" ☐

Put them in backpack ☐

Chose a free time activity to do while
waiting for the bus ☐

Reviewed By: [＿＿＿＿＿]

Figure 9. Example of a checklist for a daily routine in the school setting.

Teaching this Strategy

- When teaching the student how to initially use the checklists, select checklists for some relatively easy routines such as a "night time routine" or "ready to go home" routine. Make sure the student knows how to perform each of the components of these routines.

- The parent or teacher should develop the first few check-lists for the student. Once the checklists are made, the student should be shown the lists and told that checklists are a method for helping people remember important things. It may be helpful to explain that everyone uses lists to aid with remembering things, such as shopping lists, to do lists, etc.

- Next, have the student read the first step on the checklist and complete that step. Once the step is completed, prompt the student to check off that step. The use of verbal prompting should be limited because it is very hard to eliminate. Better prompting strategies to use are: gesture prompts, such as pointing to the next step on the list; or partial physical prompts, such as putting the student's finger on the next step. Using these prompts instead of verbal prompts will help eliminate prompt dependence.

- Prompting and reinforcers should be used until the student is successfully using the checklist, referencing each step and checking it off as he/she proceeds through to the next step.

- Once the student has the process down for using check-lists, work on getting the student to initiate the use of the checklist independently.

Remember that using the checklist is a "process." It is important that the student learn the process itself, which may require explicit instruction. Encourage the use of checklists for even the well practiced routines of the day. This will allow for the much needed practice and provide a backup support for those days when the regular routines might be interrupted.

Homework Management Systems

One of the most challenging and ongoing struggles for these students involves keeping track of homework assignments. In addition to forgetting the teacher's instructions, they often forget to bring home the needed materials to complete assignments or fail to turn them in once they are complete. The Homework Management System is a structured method for assisting the student in managing all of the information regarding school assignments.

Using a Homework Folder (Early Primary)

This system should be used starting in early elementary school, as soon as homework is being assigned. A homework folder is a simple tool that indicates what needs to be done, including the materials needed, and how much there is to do. It has a specific place to store assignments and materials and a way to indicate when the work is finished to insure that the student will complete all assignments and turn them in. In early elementary school, most homework is in the form of worksheets or small booklets, so a folder is a very practical tool to use for organizational purposes with this age group.

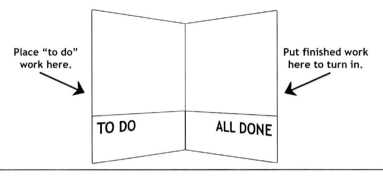

Place "to do" work here.

Put finished work here to turn in.

TO DO   ALL DONE

Figure 10: Homework folder for early primary students.

Teaching this Strategy

- The folder system should be set up with the left pocket for things that need to be done. It should be labeled "to do." The student should be taught to put the new assignments and materials into the left side of the homework folder when they are assigned. During the "end of day/ready to go home routine," the student should be taught to put the homework folder in the backpack or other designated area for take-home materials.

- At home, or in the designated home-work location, the student should get his/her homework folder from the backpack. The parent should check the folder daily to see what has been assigned, and work with the student as necessary to complete the work.

- Once the work is done, the student should be taught to put the completed work into the right pocket of the folder. That pocket should be labeled "finished work."

- The student should be taught to put the homework folder in the backpack or other designated area, such as a "to go box," as soon as the work is completed.

Using a Homework Summary Page (Late Primary)

As the student progresses through the primary grades and the assignments require the use of books and other materials, he/she should transition to a simple assignment summary page. On this worksheet, the subject, specific assignment, due date, and any materials needed to complete that assignment should be indicated (refer to Figure 11, below). Highlighting or color coding by subject area is also a necessary support to assist the student in easily identifying the needed materials. Book covers, subject folders and any other materials needed for a specific subject should all be coordinated.

Homework Summary Page (Late Primary)

SUBJECT	ASSIGNMENT	DUE	MATERIALS
Math	Pgs 21-22 odd problems	Tue. Jan 22	Math book
Spelling	Study for Test	Fri. Jan 25	Spelling list & flashcards
Science	Volcano Project for Science Fair	Fri. Feb 25	Card board, papermache, red paint, brown paint

Figure 11. Example of Homework Summary Page for late primary students. Highlighting, or color coding may be used to assist the student with identifying needed materials.

Teaching this Strategy

- The student should be taught to write down assignments and materials needed on the summary sheet as soon as each assignment is given. It is helpful for the sheet to be immediately accessible (e.g., affixed to the top of the desk).

- A teacher or aide should check the sheet initially to make sure it is complete. Provide rewards for copying down the assignments correctly and identifying the needed materials. Use a cluster organizer as necessary to help the student identify the needed materials (as described earlier in this chapter and further in Chapter 2).

- As part of the "ready to go home routine", the student should take out the homework summary sheet and get all the materials listed. It may be necessary for him/her to check off each item as he/she goes through the list to ensure he/she does not forget anything. Color coding each folder and book cover by subject helps with this process. The items should be placed in the student's backpack along with the homework summary page.

- Once home, or at the designated homework location, a homework checklist should be developed. The student will need to learn to prioritize the assignments (as dis-cussed in Chapter 3) and estimate the amount of time each assignment will take (as discussed in Chapter 2) before he can develop a home work checklist independ-ently. For now, the parent or another designated person should assist the child in prioritizing the assignments and determining "work time" for each. Once this is done, fill out a homework checklist which indicates what work they should do, for how long, and in what order. The student will utilize this checklist to complete the home-work independently.

- As assignments are completed, they should be checked off of the homework checklist.

- All materials and completed work should be placed in the student's backpack or other designated area such as the "to go box" as soon as the work is completed.

Using a Homework Summary Page (Secondary)

Students should utilize this tool when they transition to junior high and high school where they have multiple classes and teachers (refer to Figure 12).

Bright Idea
It is very helpful for teachers to write down all homework assignments on the board in a specific place each day. This makes the information visual and static, increasing the chances that the student with autism will attend to it. Another accommo-dation to consider is for the teacher to include due dates and a list of needed take home materials on the board next to the written assignment.

Period	Subject		Monday	✓	Tuesday	✓	Wednesday	✓	Thursday	✓	Friday	✓
1	Algebra	Homework:	Pgs. 33-36		Pgs. 37-39		Pgs. 40-42		Pgs. 43-45			
		Due Date:	10/18/2004	■	10/19/2004	■	10/20/2004	■		■		■
		Materials:	Book & Binder		Book & Binder		Book & Binder					
2	English	Homework:	Ch 4 Great Gasby		Ch 4 Great Gasby		Ch 4 Great Gasby					
		Due Date:	10/18/2004	■	10/19/2004	■	10/20/2004	■		■		■
		Materials:	Great Gasby		Great Gasby		Great Gasby		Great Gasby		Great Gasby	
3	Computer Science	Homework:	None		None		None		None			
		Due Date:		■		■		■		■		■
		Materials:	None		None		None					
4	Art	Homework:	None		None		None					
		Due Date:		■		■		■		■		■
		Materials:	None		None		None					
5	Spanish	Homework:	Word List Ch 3		Word List Ch 3		Word List Ch 3					
		Due Date:	Test 10/20/04	■	Test 10/20/04	■	Test 10/20/04	■		■		■
		Materials:	Book & Flashcards		Book & Flashcards		Book & Flashcards					

Figure 12. Example of Homework Summary Page for junior high student to high school.

Teaching this Strategy

- This is taught in the same way as described previously except that the student will need to learn how to complete the homework summary sheet during each class period when an assignment is given.

Time Management Systems

It is virtually impossible for most adults to remember all of the activities, appointments and special projects. that we must complete on a daily basis. To assist us with remembering, we use many strategies and supports including day planners, calendars, personal digital assistants, shopping lists, reminder notes, and the like. Did anyone explicitly teach us how and when to use these time management systems? Most of us came to these systems on our own, likely after failing to remember something which then resulted in a bad outcome. We learned which strategies to use and how to use them with no instruction from others. Many of us began by making simple lists, probably in high school or college, or we began using calendars to remember when tests were scheduled or when bills were due. When we graduated into our careers and family lives, our lists and calendars evolved to better meet our demands at that time in our lives. Our time management systems grew with us and become more "developmentally appropriate." For example, I now use several time management tools to remember all of the things I must do. I have a day planner (to keep track of my daily obligations and appointments), a family events calendar (so that I know what everyone else is doing), a home finance planner (to keep track of payments and financial obligations), a greeting card organizer (to make sure I do not forget any important occasions), and a shopping list/coupon organizer (to keep track of all the supplies needed by my family and to save money whenever possible), not to mention several reminder notes that are posted in various locations around the house, car, and office.

These strategies for remembering are an important part of our lives, yet we often do not see the importance of teaching our children how to use them. People with high functioning autism will not come to these systems without direct instruction. They must be taught how and when to use them. And, due to their inherent deficits in organization, planning, and recall, it is imperative that we begin teaching them these strategies at a very early age. I advocate teaching the use of a schedule or daily planner beginning in preschool. Of course we are not going to give a preschooler a PDA and say, "Here you go; now you are organized." We are going to provide the child with a developmentally appropriate time management system, such as an object or picture schedule and teach him/her how to effectively use it. Since the target population for this manual is elementary to adult students with high functioning autism and related disabilities, I am going to provide instruction on time management systems appropriate for that age group. This includes learning to use a monthly calendar and daily schedule (along with goal and priority worksheets which will be discussed in Chapter 3).

Case Example

Frank, an adult man with Asperger's Syndrome who I met in an adult independent living skills center, shared with me his method for remembering important things. I had a pretty good idea what the system was before he told me, because he had Post-it notes all over his notebook and sticking out of his very thick wallet. He even had a couple notes posted on his person. He told me that he writes reminders to himself about all the things he has to do. When I asked him how that was working for him he said, "Pretty good, except sometimes I have to write myself reminder notes about where I left a certain reminder note, and I sometimes run out of these Post-it notes, then I am in real trouble!"

Using a Reminder Board

A reminder board is a place to post any notes, appointment cards, Action Plan Cards (discussed in Chapter 4), or other items that will cue the student to remember important things. It is best to incorporate this into the time management system and assign a specific location so that the student does not need a reminder about where he/she keeps his/her reminders, as was the case for Frank. A designated bulletin board or white board in the student's planning zone (as discussed later in this chapter), and/or a "reminder page" in the homework management system are very good alternatives.

Teaching this Strategy

- Assign a designated "reminder board" or page in the homework management system and inform the student that this is a place to keep reminder notes.

- Provide the student with Post-it notes or appropriate writing instruments for making reminder notes.

- When there is an event that will be important for the student to remember to add to his/her time management system, prompt him/her to write a reminder and place it in the designated location. When prompting, try to use indirect prompts such as, "This will be important to remember; what should you do?" or simply point to the board or page with an expectant look. These types of prompts are far easier to fade that a direct verbal prompt such as, "Write this on your reminder board."

- Reward the student for independently putting items on the reminder board/page. Even if they later turn out to be irrelevant reminders, reward the use of the system. Some training can be done to assist the student with determining relevant vs. irrelevant reminders in the same way discussed in the earlier section on recalling information from lectures and text.

- The student will eventually need to self-manage this system. This will be discussed in later chapters. For now, simply working with him/her to develop the skills for utilizing this system will greatly improve his/her ability to recall important things and manage his/her time, as well as decrease overall feelings of stress.

Using A Monthly Calendar

The monthly calendar is used to show when regularly occurring and irregularly occurring monthly and weekly events will take place. At this point, introduce the monthly calendar by showing the student how to schedule regularly occurring and irregularly occurring routines for the month. This will help him/her to begin long-term planning and simple adjustments that are necessary in the time management process (refer to Figure 13). In the coming chapters, the monthly calendar will also be used as a tool to teach management of complex tasks, assignments, and projects as well as goals and priorities.

Teaching this Strategy

- Explain to the student that the monthly calendar will help him/her to better manage his/her time by helping him/her plan for long-term goals and activities.

- Begin by filling in all of the regularly scheduled monthly and weekly activities and routines (e.g., soccer, karate, study for spelling test).

- Next, fill in any irregular routines or activities that are scheduled for that month. This should include due dates

SEPTEMBER 2004						
Sunday	Monday	Tuesday	Wednesday	Thursday	Friday	Saturday
		1	2	3	4	5
			Soccer Practice 5:00 - 6:00		Spelling test	Soccer Game 12:00 - 1:00 **Beach Trip**
6	7	8	9	10	11	12
			Soccer Practice 5:00 - 6:00		Spelling Test	Soccer Game 8:00 - 9:00 Beach Trip 11:00
13	14	15	16	17	18	19
Beach Trip	Calculus test		Soccer Practice 5:00 - 6:00		Spelling Test	Soccer Game 9:00 - 10:00
20	21	22	23	24	25	26
			Soccer Practice 5:00 - 6:00		Spelling Test	Soccer Game 10:00 - 11:00
27	28	29	30			

Figure 13. Example of monthly planning calendar which shows regularly occurring and irregularly occurring monthly events

or deadlines for long-term projects or assignments. The student will learn (as described in the coming chapters) how to break long-term projects down into components and plot out the "work time" required for completing the steps and meeting the deadlines.

- When plugging in irregular routines, there will often need to be some adjustments made to the regularly occurring routines already on the calendar. For example, in Figure 12, the family trip to the beach scheduled for September 5th conflicted with the regular Saturday soccer routine. The calendar needed to be adjusted to reflect this schedule conflict as indicated by the bold type or Figure 12. Initially, simply point out the conflict and show the student how to make the necessary adjustments. In the chapters that follow, the skills necessary for making and adjusting the schedule will be taught.

- Make sure that the monthly calendar is kept in a handy location. This may be at the front of the school binder or in a "planning zone" at home.

Using A Daily Schedule

The daily schedule should be used to show what the student will be doing that day and in what order the activities will occur. The schedule should be made and revised each day, or the night before, based on the priorities for that day and the time estimated for each activity, as this will be discussed in Chapter 3, Prioritization. It may be helpful to have a few separate daily schedules depicting different components of the Student's day. For example, a school day

Bright Idea

When determining what type of time management system to use, consider what will be easiest for the student and any special interests or talents he/she possess. It may be helpful to present examples of different options and ask the student which he/she prefers to use. Often a computerized system/software or P.D.A. are very effective and interesting to the student.

schedule (see Figure 14a), a home afternoon/evening schedule (see Figure 14b), and a weekend schedule. Notice that there may also be task specific checklists utilized for some of the activities/tasks identified on the schedule as indicated by the (*).

The daily schedule should be an actively used tool to assist the student in completing routines and transitioning from one activity to another. The student will need to learn how to read the schedule and check off activities when they are completed. He/she will eventually need to learn to set up the daily schedule independently as discussed in Chapter 3. However, it is important that he/she first become proficient at using it.

Teaching this Strategy

- Teaching schedule-following is very similar to teaching the student to use the checklists described earlier. Initially the teacher or parent should fill out the schedule, based on what needs to be done that day. This will include regular daily routines, items from the monthly calendar and items from the reminder board. Work through

School Day Schedule		Done
(7:50 - 8:00)	*Ready for the day routine	☐
(8:05 - 8:50)	Algebra	☐
(8:55 - 9:40)	History	☐
(9:45 -10:30)	Tutorial/break	☐
(10:35 -11:20)	Biology	☐
(11:25 -12:05)	Lunch	☐
(12:10 -1:45)	Computer Science	☐
(1:50 - 2:35)	P.E.	☐
(2:35 - 2:45)	*Ready to go home routine	☐
(2:45)	Catch the bus	☐
Reviewed By:	☐	

Figure 14a. Sample Daily School Schedule for a high school student. Note that the subjects may be COLOR coded to coordinate with the folders and book covers for those subjects.

Afternoon/Evening Schedule		Done
(3:00 -4:00)	Free time	☐
(4:00 -6:00)	*Homework	☐
(6:00 -6:30)	Dinner	☐
(6:30 -7:30)	*Chores	☐
(7:30 -9:00)	Free time	☐
(9:00 -9:30)	Planning routine	☐
(9:30 -9:45)	*Night-time routine	☐
Reviewed By:	☐	

Figure 14b. Sample Afternoon/Evening Schedule for high school student. The (*) indicates routines that have corresponding checklists. Refer to Figure 8 for an example of the Night-time routine checklist that corresponds to this schedule.

the process with the student observing, and answer specific questions about why certain things need to get done. The student will eventually take over the process of filling out the schedule based on the time estimated for each activity and the priorities for the day.

- Explain to the student that schedules are a method for helping people remember important things and manage time wisely. They are used to assist us with getting things done that have to be done and still allow us to plan time to do the things that we really like to do. It may be helpful to explain that everyone uses lists and schedules to aid with time management.

- Once all of the schedule items are filled in, it is helpful to highlight any time slots that are not taken. These areas indicate "free time." The child will be able to specify a preferred activity on the daily schedule during any "free time" slots remaining on any given day. This process will help the student learn to "self reinforce" by planning in breaks or desired activities throughout the day.

- Review with the student what each activity or routine on the schedule is. Pay particular attention to any irregular routines or activities and review these in great detail. It may even be necessary to write a "Social Story" (Gray, C., 1994), role play, or practice that activity or routine with the student to better prepare him/her. Make sure to use a checklist as necessary.

- Have the student take the schedule and keep it in a location where it can readily be accessed. This may be on the desk or in the front of the school binder for the school schedule. It may be on the bedroom door or on a bulletin board, "the planning zone," at home.

- Next, have the student read the first step on the schedule and complete that step. Once the step is completed, the teacher or parent should prompt the student to check off that step. As stated previously, the use of verbal prompts should be limited because these prompts are hard to eliminate. A far better prompt is a gesture such as pointing to the activity on the schedule, or a partial physical prompt, such as putting the student's finger on the next step. If verbal prompts are used, make sure they are not direct instructions. For example, it is far better to say, "What should you be doing right now? How can you find out?" rather than saying, "Go check your schedule!"

- Prompting and reinforcements should be used until the student is successfully using the schedule for transitions and checking each step off as it is completed.

- If the student is not able to complete a designated activity in the time allotted on the schedule, an adjustment will need to be made. This should be done with the student.

- It is often necessary to eliminate some of the designated "free time" so that he/she can complete a critical task. The student should begin to see that "free time" is often eaten up by unexpected tasks or when he/she procrastinates or does not finish things in a timely manner. This realization can be quite disturbing to some individuals. He/she will need to learn how to evaluate outcomes (as described in Chapter 4) to see how making good choices and completing high priority tasks will benefit him/her in the long run, even though it may mean giving up some free time in the short run. For now, if the student has a behavior problem when "free time" is bumped, try to be empathetic ("I understand that this can be frustrating, but let's work together so you can get that free time in at another time").

Recalling and Restating: Structure

Structure includes modifications to the materials, environment or routines that will better accommodate the needs of a person. Since recalling and restating are core deficit areas for individuals on the autism spectrum, the following are specific structural modifications that will assist the student in these areas.

Establish Structured Routines

By having predictable routines that are practiced and repeated the same way over and over, recall of how to complete the steps of the routine will become easier over time.

It is important to have the student participate in the development of the routines and help create the checklists so that he/she begins to understand how to develop them independently. In addition, the student will need to learn the critical skill of how to resume a routine when an interruption occurs. This is relatively easy to teach when the student is using the checklists. The student simply learns to reference the checklist and resume the steps following the last completed (checked off) step. He/she will also need to learn how to problem-solve an unexpected situation that might arise during the course of a routine. For example, in the middle of the bedtime routine, he/she finds there is no toothpaste. This is enough to send some individuals with high functioning autism into a full blown meltdown, or at least it may prevent them from completing the routine. Strategies for how to problem solve this will be discussed in Chapters 4 and 5.

When planning the routines and developing the checklists to go with them, break these routines into daily, weekly, monthly, and irregular routines. Name each routine so that the child becomes familiar with the label so it can be plugged into the time management systems without confusion.

Daily Routines

These are routines that happen on a daily basis. They include things like getting ready for school or work, making lunch, getting ready to go home from school or work, homework routine, bedtime routine, and a ready-for-the-next-day routine. It may be important to distinguish weekend routines from weekday routines because they are typically different.

Weekly Routines

These are routines that happen regularly, but on a weekly basis. Although it is not imperative for these events to occur on the same day each week, if they do, it will help with planning and time management. For example, if the student knows that the spelling test is always on Friday, he/she can establish a weekly 20-minute study routine for Wednesday and Thursday night. If the day of the spelling test varies from week to week, the student will have a more difficult time establishing a stable routine. Some other examples of weekly routines are clean up routines such as; clean up the room routine, clean-out-the-backpack routine, clean out the refrigerator routine. Grocery shopping routine and a laundry routine are additional examples of weekly routines.

Monthly Routines

These are routines that occur regularly but only one to two times per month. Examples include: bill paying routine, boy/girl scout meeting routine, etc.

Irregular Routines

These are routines or events that occur occasionally and are not easily predictable. They include things like getting a haircut, dental appointments, doctor appointments, assembly-day routine, substitute-teacher routines, etc. These are the situations which individuals on the autism spectrum have the hardest time dealing with. By establishing a routine, developing a checklist for that routine and practicing it through role playing and or "Social Stories/Comic Strip

Conversations" (Gray, C., 1994), there will be a decrease in the anxiety and frustration that typically occurs in such situations. It is important to let the student know as far in advance as possible when one of these irregular routines is going to occur. Put it on the schedule or planner if at all possible and consider having a practice session ahead of time.

Visually Structure and Organize the Environment

It has been shown through the TEACCH program (www.teacch.com) how very important physical and visual structure are for assisting individuals with autism in functioning at their highest potential. The physical layout of an area can either promote attention and learning or detract from it. By carefully arranging the environment, we can prevent many of the behavioral issues discussed in the introduction of this book that are a result of the executive difficulties inherent in autism. The following are some specific methods for visually structuring the environment that will help to facilitate learning and recall.

Establish Zones

Establish specific zones or areas where specific tasks/routines and only those specific tasks/routines occur. Use visual parameters when setting up these zones, establishing clear boundaries to show where the area starts and where it ends. Have the materials, and only the materials needed for that specific zone task or activity, present. By having these zones established and having only needed materials present, you will be promoting recall of the specific task or routines that are supposed to be completed in that zone.

Some zones to establish in the home are: homework zone, grooming self care zone, relaxation zone, and the planning zone. Some zones to establish at school are: independent work zone, group work zone, relaxation zone. Many teachers also find it helpful to set up a ready for the day zone where students check in and access all the necessary information for participation each day.

Use Labels and Containers

Use containers to organize materials (have a place for everything). Label the containers or use pictures or icons so there is always a concrete visual reminder of where things are. Also, label the spot where that container or those materials belong. For example, label drawers indicating what belongs inside, label cupboards or shelves to show where things belong (put everything in its place). Establish "clean up routines" where the child is taught how to sort items into the appropriate containers (including a trash container) and place the containers in their appropriate places. This should begin when the child is young and the clean up routines should be expanded and made more specific as indicated in the discussion on structured routines. There should be a clean-the-room routine, clean-the-backpack routine, etc. This is an invaluable skill which will help the student with prioritizing, planning, and organizing well into adult life.

Functionally Appropriate Arrangement of Items

This may mean having duplicate items, each one placed in a location where the item is typically used. By doing this, not only will it save time, but may actually serve to "jar the memory" about what needs to be done. Putting items in locations that will prompt us to remember is very effective. I use this strategy myself by placing all of my out-going mail next to my car keys so I remember to take it with me when I leave. If I have a movie to return, I do the same

Bright Idea
It is important when using labeling that you do not make it "autism specific." Many children with high functioning autism will be resistant to the idea of doing something that makes them look different from their peers. It is better to implement this "family wide" or "classroom wide." Many teachers have commented on how effective it has been for their whole class, not simply the student with autism. Parents have told me that siblings often become more organized and the house stays neater resulting in less time spent cleaning up messes.

thing. For individuals with autism this can be done using a "To Go Box." This is a box kept by the door where items that must go with the student when he/she leaves are placed. As part of the "ready-for-the-next-day" routine, any items that need to leave the house (backpack, permission slips, lunch money, bus pass, book to return, etc.) should be placed in that box. The box should be kept in a location which is nearly impossible to miss before leaving the house. If the person drives, make sure the keys are in the box (he/she cannot get very far without them). This can be done in the classroom by using "to go" envelopes or folders, an "out box," or a cubby. The student or teacher places any items, notes, etc. that need to be taken home that day in the designated spot, which should be in a location that cannot be missed (e.g., in the backpack, next to the classroom door, etc.) Again, I recommend this procedure be implemented for the entire class, not just for the student with autism.

Task Boxes

These are boxes that contain all of the needed materials for completing a specific task or routine. For example, a bedtime routine box might contain a razor, shaving cream, pajamas, toothbrush, toothpaste, the alarm clock, and, of course, the bedtime routine checklist. By having all of the materials gathered for the specific task, the person is more likely to complete all of the steps independently. In addition, this will save time and will eliminate the possibility of the person forgetting to do a specific step in the routine. The items themselves will serve as visual reminders. Also, by having the materials pre-gathered, you prevent the student from going off task as he/she tries to gather materials.

Task boxes can be prepared for regularly occurring tasks and routines as well as irregular routines. For example, a "going to Grandma's house" box can be prepared ahead of time, even though that is not a regularly occurring event. By having the materials prearranged, much of the anxiety about the irregular routine can be decreased.

It is important for the student to learn how to identify and gather all of the needed materials for task completion independently. This will be discussed further in the following chapters.

Recalling and Restating: Supports

Supports, again, are any type of assistance from others or specific devices that will help facilitate independence. So, if we review the recommendations for recalling and re-stating from above, this will include:

- Check lists for specific tasks and structured routines in-cluding homework management systems.
- Developmentally appropriate time management systems.

- Alarms and timers (Watch-minder and Time Timer).
- Boxes and containers that are well marked and/or made for specific organizational purposes.
- Graphic organizers (cluster type).
- Committed teachers and parents who will use good behavioral teaching strategies while the student learns the R.O.P.E.S.

Chapter 2
Organization and Planning Skills

Understanding Organization and Planning Deficits in Individuals with High Functioning Autism

To say that all individuals on the autism spectrum have deficits in "organization skills" can be misleading. Organization can mean "to arrange items orderly," which is actually an area of strength and an obsessive need for some individuals on the autism spectrum. Others on the spectrum, seem to prefer chaos over meticulous order. The term "organization skill" can also mean "to make a system for doing something/planning something." The latter is the type of organization skill that is typically impaired in individuals on the autism spectrum.

The kids who seem very orderly with their items and belongings, we will call them the "meticulous type," may have an extreme need to follow a specific organizational procedure. Remember that procedural recall and knowledge is an area of strength. Simply because they follow the proce-dure does not mean that they have the ability to develop the procedure. In some cases, however, the child with autism may have been able to develop his/her system of order (e.g., he/she decided that all the red shirts go on the left and all of the blue ones on the right). If this is the case, it is probably a good sign, a sign that he/she does have some capacity for planning and making systems for doing things. For "meticulous types," their biggest problem is likely their inability to be flexible with the system and therefore they are unable to integrate new information or accept changes.

For the student on the autism spectrum who is the "disheveled type," it is necessary to provide a lot of structure, particularly organization of his or her environment to help compensate for this deficit. There is an old saying: "A place for everything and everything in its place." If we have specific places to store things and we always return them to those spaces, we save ourselves time by eliminating the need to look for items we use to complete tasks. To take this one step further, if the items needed for specific tasks were also only kept in functionally appropriate locations, we would save even more time by eliminating the need to retrieve things. This is very important for children on the autism spectrum due to their problems with organization, planning, and shifting attention. As soon as they leave the area of the task at hand to go get the items required to complete a task, the chances that they will get off track increase tremendously. Next thing you know, you need to intervene by providing additional cues and prompts. As discussed in the previous chapter, the situation can be avoided and independence facilitated by having items in contextually appropriate locations.

Thank goodness decorators are finally learning functionality. Today there are many beautiful containers and pieces of furniture specifically designed with organization in mind. Having your wares out in the open or in baskets, boxes, or crates is in fashion and it is a necessary design strategy for individuals with autism.

As indicated in the previous chapter, organization and recall cannot really be discussed as mutually exclusive. To be able to effectively recall and reproduce past actions and information, the information must be well organized at the time of learning. As discussed in the previous chapter the use of visual strategies are important for assisting individuals on the autism spectrum in the learning process. In this chapter, many of the visual strategies from the previous chapter are broken down even further to teach students a system for organizing information and making action plans so that they can effectively plan and complete complex activities and routines.

The Operational Definition of Organization and Planning

The ability to define a goal or task and break the task down into manageable components, identify and get the needed resources and/or materials for completing the task, and completing the designated steps within the time allotted.

Organization and Planning: Strategies

Strategies, are those behaviors and skills that are taught to help a person overcome or compensate for his/her deficits. In the following section some strategies for helping individuals with high functioning autism overcome and/or compensate for deficits in organization and planning will be discussed.

Case Example

Nathaniel, our "noncompliant" child from the previous chapter, became very good at recalling the chores his mother told him to do. He was able to complete many of them independently once he learned how to use the cluster organizer to recall the instructions. His mom indicated that he was still having a difficult time with many of the more complex tasks, and she could not figure out why. For example, he would do great with taking out the trash, unloading the dishwasher, and taking care of the family dog. He really struggled with chores like cleaning his room or cleaning the bathroom. "He picks up stuff on the floors or counters, but does not do a thorough job," his mother indicated.

When I sat down with Nathaniel to figure out the problem, I asked him, "What does it mean to unload the dishwasher?" He answered by saying, "You open the dishwasher up and put the glasses away, then the plates and bowls, then the silverware, then anything else that is left." I then asked him, "What does it mean to clean your room?" He answered, "You put stuff away." It became very clear that he needed much more practice using the strategy for breaking tasks down, particularly more complex task.

Graphic Organizers
Using Graphic Organizers to Break Down Complex Tasks & Assignments

Complex tasks are those which are made up of many smaller sub-tasks. The more sub-tasks there are to a given task or assignment, the more "complex" it is. Many individuals with high functioning autism can organize and plan simple tasks, but fall apart when they are forced to deal with complex tasks. A cluster organizer can be used to help a student break down complex tasks so that he/she can manage them more effectively (see the example in Figure 15).

**Graphic Organizer for
Breaking Instructions Down**

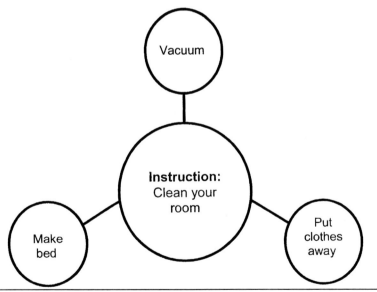

Figure 15: Example of how a graphic organizer was used to assist Nathaniel in breaking down a complex instruction (clean your room) into more manageable sub-tasks.

Teaching this Strategy

- Using the cluster type organizer, first identify the complex task to be completed and write it in the middle bubble.

- Teach the student how to identify the components or sub-tasks of that complex task following the procedure for using graphic organizers to recall instructions as described in Chapter 1 (refer to pages 36 and 37).

- Order does not matter at this point, simply getting the student to state all of the pieces of the complex task are essential.

- It may be necessary to break down some of the identified sub-skills into smaller, more manageable components. Continue adding arms and bubbles as needed, while prompting the student to identify the steps of each sub-skill.

- Practice this procedure often and with a variety of complex skills including chores, recreational projects, school assignments, etc. This will promote generalization and decrease frustration when the student is faced with novel complex tasks.

- The eventual goal is for the student to break down complex tasks into simple, doable components independently. He/she may become independent at completing the graphic organizer, or may even begin to "think through" the process. Regardless of the method acquired, the student will decrease his/her dependence on other people and be less frustrated with the demands placed on him/her once this process is learned.

Sequencing Steps of a Complex Task and Assignments

Once the steps of a complex task or set of instructions have been identified, the student will need to put them in a sequential order, the process for doing the steps. This can be done using a sequential organizer like the one in Figure 16 below.

Sequencing Steps of a Task

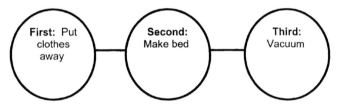

Figure 16: Example of a sequential organizer used to put the steps of an instruction in order after the instruction had been broken down (see Figure 15).

Teaching this Strategy

- To teach this step, show the student the sequential organizer, with the correct number of bubbles, and ask, "Which step should be done first, next and last?" As the student calls out the steps, have him/her write them in the appropriate bubble on the sequential organizer. It is also helpful to have the student cross the items off of the cluster organizer once they are transferred to a checklist or computer. This will help him/her see what steps still remain.

- It is important for the student to learn how to evaluate consequences for completing the steps in order, which will be discussed in later chapters. For now, simply assist the student in recognizing his/her sequencing errors and why his/her plan is flawed. This can be done through probing questions and error correction. In the example provided in Figure 16, Nathaniel needed to put his clothes in the drawers first because they were on the bed and floor. The location of the clothes would have prevented him from making the bed and vacuuming the floor, or he would have had the unnecessary steps of moving the clothes out of the way. When I discussed cleaning the room with Nathaniel, he indicated, "First I should vacuum." I responded with a probing question, "If you start with vacuuming, what will be in your way?" "If the clothes are in your way for vacuuming and making your bed, what is the best step to start with?"

NOTE: Once the student is able to break down tasks inde-pendently, he/she is essentially able to make his/her own checklist. This essential process is a critical life skill that can easily be taught using these simple visual techniques.

Using Graphic Organizers to Identify Needed Materials

An important piece of organization and planning is the ability to identify and get all of the resources or materials needed for completing a specific task. Figure 17 illustrates the use of a cluster organizer to break down a homework assignment and determine the needed materials.

Case Example

Alan, our very smart student from the previous chapter, learned how to pull out the important components from his reading and from class lectures using the cluster organizer. His test scores in social studies and science improved tremendously as a result. His teacher, Mrs. Gunther, was still concerned that he was not doing as well as he could be. He often failed to turn in homework assignments, even in his favorite subject, math. They began a communication book between school and home in order to track assignments. What they discovered was that often Alan would know what the assignment was, but would fail to recognize the materials he needed to bring home to complete the assignment. As a result, he would not do the work and then get a zero.

Graphic Organizers for Identifying Needed Materials

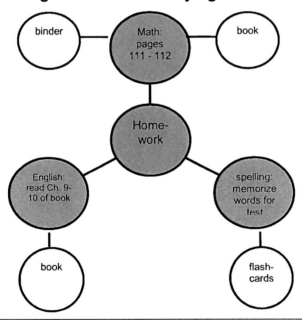

Figure 17. In this example, the homework task was first broken into its component pieces (shaded bubbles). Then the graphic organizer was expanded to show what materials were needed for each component (white bubbles).

Teaching this Strategy

- Have the student complete a cluster organizer for recalling and/or breaking down the specific instructions or assignments given, as taught in Chapter 1.

- Next, have him/her expand the organizer by adding bubbles for needed materials. The bubbles should be added initially by the instructor, who will prompt the student with increasingly specific questions until he/she is able to identify the needed materials. For example you might say, "Your assignment is math, pages 111-112. What materials will you need to complete this assignment?" If the student answers correctly by stating the necessary materials, reward the student. If the student is unable to answer correctly, make the question more specific, such as, "Do you need a specific book? Which one?" These probing questions should become less specific as the student is able to identify the needed materials.

- Eventually the student will be responsible for completing the entire graphic organizer for identifying needed materials independently.

Bright Idea

If a student is having trouble using the graphic organizer to identify task components and materials, the instructor may need to take a step back and work on breaking down tasks and sequencing steps using more concrete visual aids.

NOTE: These are also very good skills to work on with early learners (pre-k through age 8).

- Take photos of the student completing specific functional tasks that are part of the daily routines. For example, for the task of making a peanut butter and jelly sandwich, have pictures of the child completing each step of the task; opening bread package, taking out a slice, opening peanut butter jar, getting peanut butter on knife, spreading peanut butter on bread, etc.

- Give the student a pile of pictures for a specific task, out of order. Teach the student to put the pictures in order.

- When he/she learns to successfully put the pictures in order, make it a bit harder by having certain pictures missing. Have the student tell you what steps are missing from the sequence.

- Once he/she can do this, teach the student to verbally state the steps of the sequence. To teach this, hold the pictures where the student cannot see them. Place one card in the sequence on the table (it helps to begin at the first step on the first few trials). Have him/her ask for the picture of the step that comes next (without seeing it). This procedure can also be done using backward chaining. Lay all of the pictures out except that final picture, and have the student identify only the last step. Continue this strategy until the child is able to verbally indicate the next step no matter where the sequence is started.

Effective Planning and Time Management

A critical skill in effective planning and time management is estimation. To schedule any activity, you must first be able to determine or estimate the amount of time it will take you. It is only then that you can plug that activity into the rest of your schedule. We are able to easily predict about how long a particular task will take us based on our previous experience with that task. For example, I know that I need to allow myself one hour to complete my morning routine. Individuals with autism often have a very difficult time judging how long activities will take to complete, even known routines. In addition, due to their attention problems, they often get off track, and a task that should have taken only 15 minutes ends up taking much longer.

Novel tasks or situations are a little harder to predict. However, we are usually able to "guesstimate" the amount of time even a novel activity will take by recalling a similar task or situation and how long that took us. For example, I have never had a pedicure, but I have had a manicure. So I can "guesstimate" that a pedicure will take about 45 minutes since that is about how long a manicure takes. Guesstimation is fairly easy for us to do since we are able to see the relationships, similarities and differences, between novel situations and previous situations. As discussed in Chapter 1, individuals with autism do not integrate information and recognize relationships the same way most people do, so this skill must be directly taught.

Time Estimation

Start estimation by working with the student on known tasks and activities. The student will need to check his/her estimation skills and practice them as necessary. This can be accomplished by keeping a "Time Journal" (refer to the example in Figure 18). The Time Journal serves four functions. First, it will help to establish how long certain tasks and activities take to complete. Once a fairly comprehensive log is established in writing, the student will be able to refer to it to estimate the amount of time to allocate for specific tasks. He/she can plug them into the daily schedule or calendar without requiring help from others. Second, this Time Journal will provide a list of activities to draw from when the student must learn how to "guesstimate" the amount of time required for novel tasks and activities. Third, it will provide practice and an opportunity to see how good or bad the student is at estimation. The student will be able to compare how long he/she thought a task would take to how long it actually took. Over time and with practice, he/she should become increasingly better at estimation. Lastly, the Time Journal will be a valuable tool in helping improve efficiency. When tasks take longer than expected the student will learn to evaluate why by identifying the biggest competing behaviors and environmental distractions and then develop plans for improving efficiency at these tasks (as will be covered in Chapter 5, Self-Management).

Activity	Estimation	Start Time	End Time	Total time	Difference
Morning Routine	45 minutes	7:00	8:15	1 hr 15 min	(+) 30 minutes
Chores	20 minutes	5:00	5:30	30 minutes	(+) 10 minutes
Dinner	30 minutes	6:00	6:20	20 minutes	(-) 10 minutes
Homework Routine	60 minutes	3:30	5:00	1 hr 30 minutes	(+) 30 minutes
Bedtime Routine	20 minutes	8:30	9:15	45 minutes	(+) 25 minutes

Figure 18: Example of Time Journal used to estimate the amount of time daily activities might take. The student should utilize this to become proficient at estimation and in order to plan activities in his/her daily schedule.

Teaching this Strategy

- Begin by explaining to the student the purpose(s) of the Time Journal.

- Assist the student in filling in each of the activities to be measured. These should be tasks or routines from the daily schedule that are familiar to the student. Do not use novel or irregular routines at first.

- Have the student estimate how long each of these tasks or routines should take to complete. Do not provide any prompting in the initial sessions. Let the student come up with an estimate on his/her own. If he/she is unable to answer, provide some parameters by asking, "Does that take you more than an hour, less than an hour, less than 30 minutes?" Write the estimation in the journal.

- The student should complete the tasks, filling in the start and end times for the specified activities as he/she completes the routines. The actual logging may require some direct prompting from a teacher or parent. It may help to add a "log in Time Journal" step to the task/routine checklists described in Chapter 1 to cue the student to perform this new step.

- At the end of the day, have the student fill in the total time and difference columns. Any estimation that was less than 10 minutes off is great! Provide a lot of praise and a reinforcer for these close estimations. Discuss with the student those estimations that were off by more than 10 minutes.

- For gross overestimations (i.e., student estimated that it would take far longer than it actually did), point out that he/she was more efficient then he/she thought he/she would be at that task. Ask if there was anything that contributed to his/her being able to complete the task quickly. This will introduce the concept of "efficiency" which will be elaborated on later.

- For gross underestimations (i.e., student estimated that it would take far less time than it did), point out that he/she was not as efficient at that task as he/she thought he/she would be. Ask what things occurred that might have decreased efficiency, such as distractions, lack of motivation to do the task, etc.

The goal of this activity is for the student to be able to estimate approximately 80 percent of his/her known routines and tasks with no more than 10 minute differences between estimation and actual time. It is okay for the student to refer to previous pages in the Time Journal when making new estimations; in fact this should be encouraged at first because this teaches him/her to base estimates on past experiences.

Time "Guesstimation"

Guesstimating is what we do when we are forced to determine how much time we think that a new or novel task or situation will take. It is difficult and often we are incorrect and have to make adjustments accordingly. For example, if I guesstimated that my pedicure would take 45 minutes and it actually took two hours, I might have to cancel or postpone my next scheduled appointment. Adjusting the schedule is a necessary skill that we need to teach at a later point. For now, we will focus our teaching on "guesstimating" and drawing these guesses from previous experiences.

As discussed above, we often base our guesstimates on previous experiences that are similar to, but not exactly the same as, the current situation. This is not something that comes naturally for students with autism. We can teach this valuable skill through the use of the Time Journal and graphic organizers such as the Venn diagram (refer to Figure 19.

Teaching this Strategy

- Once the student has successfully completed the Time Journal with eighty percent accuracy in estimation of known tasks and routines, he/she can begin to "guesstimate."

- Present the Venn diagram and show the student how to use it to compare and contrast activities. If he/she is unfamiliar with a Venn diagram, practice using it with easy comparisons (such as comparing a cat and a dog). If he/she is familiar with the Venn, have him/her use it to compare the new activity to a previous activity from the Time Journal.

Venn Diagram for Comparing Activities

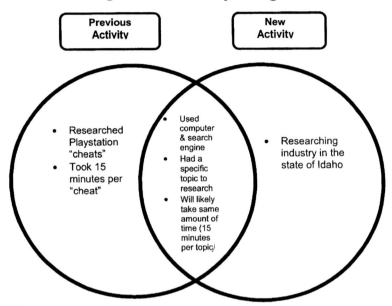

Figure 19. In this example, the student used a Venn Diagram to compare the novel situation (researching the industry in the state of Idaho) to a previous similar experience (researching Playstation cheats) which he had logged in his Time Journal. He was able to draw a comparison from that previous experience and make a "guesstimate" of how much time to allot for the novel task.

- Fill in the name of the novel task. Have the student go to the Time Journal and pick an activity that he/she thinks is most similar to the new activity. Once he/she has selected the activity, write it on the "previous experience" loop of the Venn diagram. Have the student describe the two tasks, plugging in the similarities in the overlapping section and the differences in the non-overlapping sections. Make sure to include how much time the known previous activity took to complete. Based on the comparison, the student should be able to "guesstimate" how much time the novel task might take.

- If the student is having a hard time choosing one appropriate similar activity from the Time Journal, the instructor may need to narrow it down to two possible activities from the Time Journal that are similar to the novel task. The student should then do a comparison with each activity using the Venn diagram, as described above.

- Once the comparisons are complete, the student should be able to determine which task is the "most" similar to the novel task. With practice, he/she will learn to identify the most similar task from the Time Journal independently.

- The student can fine tune "guesstimation" skills the same way he/she did with estimation. This involves tracking guesstimates on the Time Journal and comparing them to the actual time. A reasonable goal for this skill should be for the student to come within fifteen minutes about eighty percent of the time.

Estimating/Guesstimating
"Work Time" for Complex Tasks

For complex tasks, such as a term paper, book report, model airplane, etc., it is necessary to break the task down and determine the "work time" for completing each of the steps or sub-tasks. This procedure is a combination of many of the procedures discussed so far in this manual. The example in Figures 20a to 20f illustrates the steps involved in writing a term paper.

Teaching this Strategy

- Start by having the student divide the task into manageable pieces using a cluster organizer (refer to step 1, Figure 20a).

- Next, have the student put the steps in order using a sequential organizer (refer to step 2, Figure 20b).

- The student will need to identify all of the needed materials and resources for completing the steps of the task(s). This is done using an expansion of the cluster organizer as illustrated in step 3, Figure 20c.

- The student will then need to complete the procedure for estimating, or guesstimating how long each of the sub-tasks will require or the work time needed.

- The estimated or guesstimated "work time" should be written on the sequential organizer in the appropriate bubble (refer to step 4, Figure 20d). This information will be utilized when plotting out the steps on the monthly calendar, discussed in the next section, and when developing the daily schedule.

Calendaring and Plotting

Thus far parents or teachers have likely been completing the monthly calendar and daily schedule for the student. Although the student should have observed the process, he/she has probably had limited input into the development of these time management systems. Now that the student has a strategy to determine how long tasks, including complex tasks, should take to complete, he/she can learn to independently develop the monthly calendar including plotting out complex tasks and activities.

Developing the Monthly Calendar

The student should assume the responsibility of developing the monthly calendar at the beginning of each month. He/she will do this just as the parent or teacher did; plugging in all of the regularly occurring routines first, followed by any irregularly occurring routines, including due dates for the task and sub-tasks discussed above. As the student assumes responsibility for filling out the calendar, the parent or teacher role is to monitor the student's accuracy and provide prompting and feedback as needed until he/she becomes competent at filling out the monthly calendar.

Teaching this Strategy

- During the last planning session of the month, pull out the monthly calendar for the coming month.

- Have the student first fill in all of the regularly occurring routines. If he/she needs assistance, use indirect verbal prompts to refer him to the previous month's schedule, as opposed to giving the student the needed information, which will promote dependence. For example, say "Johnny, where can you look to get that information?" as opposed to, "Johnny, write down your soccer practices on Wednesdays."

- Next have the student plug in any irregular routines that need to be scheduled that month. He/she can pull these from the homework management system, or from the reminder board/page. Again, try to provide indirect verbal prompts, rather than giving him/her the information.

- If there is a scheduling conflict, an irregular routine interferes with a regular routine; prompt the student to make the necessary adjustment to the calendar. Remember that prioritization has not yet been taught (this is covered in Chapter 3), so he/she may have difficulty determining what an appropriate adjustment is. Suggest a couple of alternative ways to adjust the calendar and allow the student to choose. This will give him/her some sense of control and, hopefully, prevent problems.

Plotting Out Steps for Complex Tasks and Assignments

Plotting involves scheduling out the due dates and work time required for complex or multi-component tasks. For an example, refer to step 5, Figure 20e.

Teaching this Strategy

- When plotting, the student should start by plugging in the final deadlines and/or due dates of the sub-components on the monthly calendar.

- Next he/she should go through the monthly calendar and plug in the estimated "work times" for each component of the task.

- The dates that the work time is scheduled will depend on the number of days or slots on the monthly calendar available between the assignment date and the due dates or final deadline.

- It may be necessary to make adjustments to the calendar if there is a scheduling conflict (i.e., there are not enough timeslots available to complete the estimated work before the due date). If this occurs, explain to the student that he/she may need to "bump" an activity so that he/she can meet the deadline. Work with the student to re-schedule the activity that was bumped, if at all possible, for a later date on the monthly calendar. This will visually show the student that the activity is not gone, simply put off until a later date. By seeing this concretely on the monthly calendar, severe frustration can often be avoided.

- Ongoing adjustments may need to be made during the daily planning routine to insure deadlines for important tasks are met. For example, if the student was not able to complete a component of a project in the amount of work time estimated, it may be necessary to bump some free time, or other low priority activity, from the daily schedule so that the work can be completed that day. The parent or teacher should make the adjustment when filling out the daily schedule, and explain to the student why the adjustment was necessary. When possible, suggest a couple of alternative ways to adjust the daily schedule and allow the student to choose the final adjustment.

Making a Written Plan/Checklist

Now that the student has the ability to break down complex tasks into manageable steps, identify all of the needed resources and materials, and estimate of the amount of time required to complete the task, all that he/she needs to do is create a checklist to assist with recall of the well organized plan. For this, the information outlined in the above organizers are simply transferred to a simple checklist such as the R.O.P.E.S. Organization and Planning Worksheet (see example in step 6, Figure 20f).

Case Example:

I recently worked with a student, Jeff, who was very resistant to going through the planning process every day. I was able to draw on his previous experiences with learning new skills to motivate him to learn planning and time management. I asked him if his mom still tied his shoes. He said, "No, of course not!" I asked him if he always knew how to tie his shoes or if this was a skill he needed to learn. He said, "I needed to learn it, but it was not easy." I then asked him if it still took him as long to tie his shoes as it did when he first learned. He said, "Well, no. I am pretty fast at it now." I pointed out that at the time, it would have been easier to just have his mom continue tying his shoes, but that would look silly now. We then sketched out a Venn diagram comparing learning shoe tying with learning time management skills. He understood the comparison! Now he is motivated to learn these skills so he can be as independent and successful as possible as an adult. Getting buy in can be very challenging, but it is critical if the student is going to adopt these new habits and procedures teachers and parents should be diligent with their explanations and reinforcement for using these new skills.

Bright Idea

Many students are initially resistant to going through all of the steps necessary to plan and organize effectively. This resistance comes from many sources, including: a lack of understanding of these complex processes, inappropriate teaching and support in the past which has resulted in anxiety and frustration, or resistance to "wasting time" learning these new skills. It is very important for them to see the value in learning these skills. This can be done by letting them know the long-term outcome is ultimately more "free time" to engage in their preferred activities. Draw from their past experiences with learning new skills. Point out that any new skill takes longer at first, but a person does it faster as he/she gets better at it.

Review

Let's walk through the steps of planning and organizing using this common complex task, a term paper.

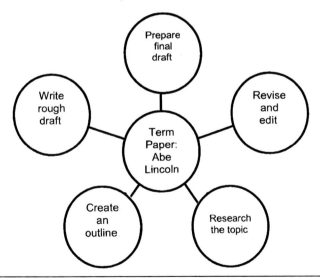

Step 1 (Figure 20a): Identify task components or subtasks using a cluster organizer.

Step 2 (Figure 20b.): Put the components in order using a sequential organizer.

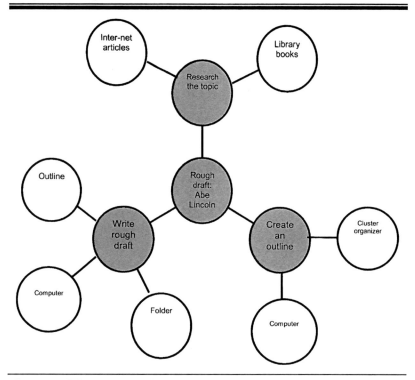

Step 3 (Figure 20c.): Identify needed materials and resources using an expanded cluster organizer.

Step 4 (Figure 20d.): Estimate the amount of time needed to complete each component.

SEPTEMBER 2004						
Sunday	Monday	Tuesday	Wednesday	Thursday	Friday	Saturday
		1	2	3	4	5
		Research Lincoln 3:00 - 5:00	**Research Lincoln 3:00 - 4:00** Soccer Practice 5:00 - 6:00	Study Spelling	Spelling test Free time 4:00 - 6:00	Soccer Game 12:00 - 1:00 Beach Trip cancelled
6	7	8	9	10	11	12
Research Lincoln 3:00 - 5:00 Beach Trip cancelled	**Write outline for Lincoln Report 4:00 - 6:00**	**Outline for Lincoln Due**	Study Calculus Soccer Practice 5:00 - 6:00	Study Spelling Study Calculus	Spelling Test Free time 4:00 - 6:00	Soccer Game 8:00 - 9:00 Beach Trip 11:00
13	14	15	16	17	18	19
Beach Trip Study Calculus	Calculus test **Work on Lincoln rough draft 5:00 - 6:00**	**Work on Lincoln rough draft 4:00 - 6:00**	Study Spelling Soccer Practice 5:00 - 6:00	**Rough draft for Lincoln Report Due** Study Spelling	Spelling Test Free time 4:00 - 6:00	Soccer Game 9:00 - 10:00 Soccer Picnic 1:00 - 4:00
20	21	22	23	24	25	26
Work on Book Report 9:00 - 12:00 Movies 2:00 - 5:00	Work on Book Report 4:00 - 6:00	Work on Book Report 4:00 - 6:00	Study Spelling Soccer Practice 5:00 - 6:00	Book Report Due Study Spelling	Spelling Test Free time 4:00 - 6:00	Soccer Game 10:00 - 11:00
27	28	29	30			
Revisions to Lincoln Report 9:00-12:00	Prepare final Lincoln Report 5:30 - 6:00 Dr. Apt 3:30	**Final Draft for Lincoln Report Due**	Study Spelling Soccer Practice 5:00 - 6:00			

Step 5 (Figure 20e.): Plot out the steps including due dates and work time on the monthly calendar. The bold type indicates components of the Abe Lincoln Report, all other information are regularly and irregularly occurring events and other complex assignments that were previously scheduled (refer back to Figure 12).

105

R.O.P.E.S. Organization and Planning Worksheet

Task

Research Abe Lincoln for history term paper.

Desired Outcome:

Get a B or better. Create and turn in outline on time.

Outcome if Not Completed:

Poor Grade, will get behind on the term paper and lose free time.

Materials Needed:

Library Books (3)

Internet articles (3)

☺ Who	I stay after school and do research. Dad picks me up from the library.
⏱ When	Sept. 1, and Sept. 2
♠Where	At school library.

	Steps:	
1	Look in card catalog for books on Abe Lincoln.	☐
2	Go to that area.	☐
3	Choose books that have good information on his life and presidency.	☐
4	Go to the computer.	☐
5	Long onto the internet.	☐
6	Type in search for Abe Lincoln, life and presidency.	☐
7	Select 3 articles.	☐
8	Print articles.	☐
9	Put articles in my purple Able Lincoln Report Folder.	☐
10	Check books out from the librarian.	☐
11	Put books in backpack to take home.	☐
12	Read books and fill out cluster organizer on each.	☐
13	Read each internet article and fill out cluster organizer on each.	☐
14	Compare all information in cluster organizers (notes) and identify 3 key points about his life and presidency.	☐
15	Write outline.	☐

Step 6 (Figure 20f.): Make a written plan/checklist for the task or task components to facilitate recall and organization. In this example, a checklist for researching the topic was developed.

With the process laid out in a very sequential order, it does not seem that complicated to teach (does it?).

Organization and Planning: Structure

Remember that structure includes modifications to the materials, environment or routines that will better accommodate the needs of a person. The structures discussed in Chapter 1 on recalling and restating will also help accommodate deficits in organization and planning skills. The following are some additional suggestions to help specifically with issues of organization and planning.

Planning and Time Management Routines
Planning Routines in the Home Setting

It is critical to establish routines for planning and time management. One routine to establish in the home is a "weekly planning session" that takes place on the same day each week. During this session the monthly calendar and goals/priorities should be reviewed and revised as necessary. There should also be a daily routine established for planning purposes. This could be a "ready-for-the-next-day" routine. Each evening the priorities for the next day are reviewed and the schedule for the next day is established. These routines provide the valuable teaching opportunities needed and establish good organization habits.

Planning Routines in the School Setting

Routines for planning and time management should also be established at school. A "school-day-preparation" routine which takes place at the beginning of the school day and a "ready-to-go-home" routine which takes place at the end of the school day are critical. In the "school-day-preparation" a school schedule for that day is developed and the priorities for the day are determined. In the "ready to go home" routine, the homework management system is reviewed and all the assignments and needed materials are collected.

Planning Zones
In the Home

It is helpful to establish a planning zone at home where the monthly calendar, reminder board, goals and priorities, and daily schedules are posted. This zone could be set up in the child's room or as part of his/her "homework zone".

At School

Rather than posting the calendars and schedules at school, establish a planning folder or section in the student's binder. This section should contain the monthly calendar, reminder page, goals and priorities, daily schedule, and the homework management system as well as copies of any graphic organizers (visual notes) or other worksheets needed for self-management.

Organization and Planning: Supports

Remember that supports are assistance from others or specific devices that will help facilitate independence. Again, many of the supports identified in Chapter 1 for recalling and restating will also assist with organization and planning. The following are supports suggested for assisting with organization and planning:

- Cluster organizers
- Sequential organizers
- Venn diagrams
- Time management systems
- Task boxes
- Check lists and appropriate worksheets
- Committed teachers and parents who will use good behavioral teaching strategies while the student learns the R.O.P.E.S.

Chapter 3

Prioritization Skills and Goal Directed Behavior

Understanding Prioritization Deficits and the Lack of Goal Directed Behavior in Individuals with High Functioning Autism

When setting goals, we do so based on timelines and the potential outcomes of our actions. We are constantly comparing tasks on our "to do lists" and evaluating them based on potential outcomes and due dates. Those items that are pressing and have big payoffs or punishment are usually considered the most urgent. Those items that do not have an impending due date or which have relatively little payoff tend to get pushed to the bottom of our priority list. It is our ability to think through the situation-action-potential outcome continuum that helps us to set our goals and priorities. By determining what the potential outcome of completing or failing to complete a task will be, we are able to make decisions and engage in goal directed behaviors.

Many people with autism are described as very "egocentric" never caring about what others think or about the outcomes of their behaviors. People on the autism spectrum are often unable to see the relationship between their actions and the consequences that ensue. They do not see that they are responsible for, or have some control over, determining outcomes. Instead, they see things that happen as acts upon them by others. For example, if a child with autism gets grounded for neglecting to take out the trash; his likely reaction is to blame the parent for grounding him rather than seeing that the grounding was a direct result of his action or lack thereof.

Is this dis-connect a characteristic of autism or due to deficits in executive function? It appears to be the latter. The inability to sequence out and organize in their thoughts along the situation-action-outcome continuum makes it very challenging for people on the autism spectrum to evaluate the potential outcomes of their actions ahead of time. Furthermore, their inability to compare previous situations and outcomes to current ones leads to a lack of learning from past contingencies, or a lack of generalized learning. These deficits in evaluation skills make it next to impossible for people with autism to effectively set goals and engage in goal directed behavior.

In Chapter 4, details about how to teach evaluation skills are presented in depth. In this chapter, exposure to the basic "Thinking Tool" is presented. The student learns to use this tool through real life examples which lay the foundation for these evaluation skills. This chapter also focuses on beginning goal setting and prioritization skills through the use of graphic organizers and a decision matrix. Learning these processes will increase the student's ability to see the relationship between actions and outcomes, which is necessary for goal directed behavior.

The Operational Definitions of Prioritization Skills and Goal Directed Behavior

Prioritization skills are the ability to rank tasks and sequence tasks by "importance" based on the potential positive or negative outcomes that will result from the completion or non-completion of the task by the deadline. Goal directed behavior is the ability to follow through with prioritized action plans to obtain desired outcomes.

Prioritization Skills and Goal Directed Behavior: Strategies

Strategies are those behaviors and skills that are taught to help a person overcome or compensate for skill deficits. In the following section some strategies for helping individuals with high functioning autism overcome and/or compensate for deficits in prioritization will be discussed.

Teaching the Situation-Action-Outcome Continuum: The Basic "Thinking Tool"

As mentioned in the introduction for this chapter, the dis-connect between situation, action and outcome is typical for individuals with autism. To most effectively set goals and priorities, one must develop an understanding of this contin-uum. This sequential relationship can be visually represented using a sequential graphic organizer that I call the basic "Thinking Tool." To further help the student distinguish between the components of this continuum, visual clarity is utilized in this specific sequential organizer (Cafferata, G., 2002). Figure 21 provides an example of this basic "Thinking Tool," which will introduce the student to this situation-action-outcome continuum. This basic process will be greatly ex-panded upon in Chapter 4, Evaluation.

Teaching this Strategy

- It is essential for the student to begin to see the nature of this continuum through real life examples, so start by showing the student how a desired outcome, a reward, for example was obtained using this model.

- First have the student identify something desirable that he/she earned. This can be a reward, a grade, an award or trophy, etc. Have him/her write it in the outcome (triangle) portion of the "Thinking Tool" worksheet

The Basic "Thinking Tool"

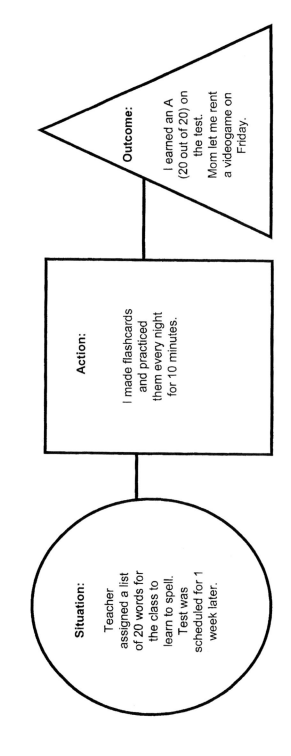

Situation:

Teacher assigned a list of 20 words for the class to learn to spell. Test was scheduled for 1 week later.

Action:

I made flashcards and practiced them every night for 10 minutes.

Outcome:

I earned an A (20 out of 20) on the test. Mom let me rent a videogame on Friday.

Figure 21. Example of the model which illustrated for the student how his actions in this situation resulted in a particular outcome.

- Have the student identify the actions needed to obtain that reward or outcome. This information is written in the actions (square) portion of the worksheet.

- Have the student identify the situation in which he/she was expected to perform the action. This information is written in the situation (circle) section of the worksheet.

- Show the student how the sequence occurred. "The situation was this (circle), the action you chose was this (square) and the outcome was this (triangle)."

- Point out the sequential nature of the continuum (first, next, last) so the student sees the relationship between the components and time. As a strategy for encouraging generalization of this process, repeat this activity often and in context whenever a reward is earned or a successful outcome is achieved.

Establishing Goal Directed Behavior

Goals are desired outcomes, including avoidance of problems. Using the "Thinking Tool", goals are the triangle or desired outcome. Once we identify our goals, we break the steps down and prioritize the things we need to do (square) to accomplish those goals. Because students with autism have a difficult time predicting outcomes and often do not even think about the potential outcomes of their behavior, they often base their choices on immediate gratification instead of choosing behaviors based on long-term outcomes or goals. Because of deficits in planning and organization, they often fail to engage in goal directed behavior, even when they can identify a desired outcome.

Short Term Goal Setting

Setting short term goals is relatively easy once the student has mastered the use of the basic "Thinking Tool." Essentially now the student must use this tool to plan for upcoming events rather than simply evaluating past events. The triangle in the "Thinking Tool" is the desired outcome or the goal that the student wants to achieve. The square is the action plan or steps the student must perform in order to obtain the outcome. The circle provides clarification about the timeline and setting conditions for performing the actions to obtain the goal.

Teaching this Skill:

- Have the student identify a reward they want to earn, this is their goal. Write the reward in the triangle of the "Thinking Tool". Identify this reward as the "Goal" the student wants to obtain.

- Have the student identify the behaviors or actions he/she must do in order to earn the reward. Be specific. For example if the reward is going to the movies on Saturday and the actions the student must perform in order to earn that reward are to complete his/her daily chore list Monday - Friday, this should be indicated in the square.

- Finally, have the student identify any specifics regarding the timeline or situations in which he/she would perform the actions. In this example, the circle might say, "Mom will give me a daily list of chores that I am expected to complete before bed each day."

- Allow the student to use the "Thinking Tool" as needed during the timeline and remind him/her of the action – outcome relationship.

- Repeat the use of the "Thinking Tool" for earning specific rewards several times and review it each time the student reaches a goal and earns the stated rewards. If some-thing occurs where the student does not earn the reward, review what occurred to prevent attainment of the goal. For example, if this student failed to complete the chores on Thursday, this failure to complete the action resulted in a loss of the reward. It is important for the student to identify this part of the process and see how the action - outcome relationship exists.

- Move into setting goals for less reinforcing items and events or those that are further off or that have more steps. When you move into longer term goals, it is critical to review where the student is at on attainment of the goal on a regular basis. The "Thinking Tool" is the student's reminder of the goal and what he/she needs to do to earn or obtain it. It should be readily accessible and reviewed regularly.

Long Term Goal Setting

Goal setting is an essential step in teaching these students to think about their choices and the long-term implications of those choices. The Goals Worksheet (refer to Figure 22) is a graphic organizer designed to help the student identify things he/she must complete and things that he/she wants to complete in a given period of time. Once the items have been identified using the goals worksheet, they can be organized and prioritized. Finally the student can develop a goal directed action plan to obtain the desired outcomes.

Teaching this Strategy

- During the first planning session of the month, have the student start by filling out the Goals Worksheet with all of the items that he/she would like to accomplish or needs to complete that month. The identified items do not need to be in order of importance at this point. Do not criticize or evaluate the items the student puts on the Goals Worksheet; for example, if the student wants to put, "Beat brother's high score on Playstation" on his list, do not judge or criticize.

- The student should pull items from the homework management system, the reminder board, as well as the previous month's list of goals that were not completed. It is fine for the parent or teacher to prompt the student about any additional items that should be on the Goals Worksheet, but, again, avoid criticizing.

Goals Worksheet

Figure 22. Example of a monthly Goals Worksheet completed by a student.

- Once the student has filled out the Goals Worksheet, he/she must evaluate the items so they can be prioritized and put in sequential order. This can be done using the Decision Matrix for Prioritization, which will be introduced next.

The Decision Matrix for Prioritization

As discussed, we typically prioritize items based on their potential outcomes (penalty or bonus) as well as the urgency (how close or far the deadline is). Once these determinations have been made, we assign a "value" to the items and compare them to other goals so that we can determine the order in which we should address them. The Decision Matrix for Prioritization is a visual representation of how to evaluate priorities (refer to Figure 23). It will assist the student with assigning some value to the items identified on the Goals Worksheet so that they can be ranked effectively.

Decision Matrix for Prioritization

	Heavy Bonus or Penalty Outcome	No or Light Bonus or Penalty Outcome
Urgent Deadline	HIGH PRIORITY • BOOK REPORT (100 POINTS) • STUDY FOR CALCULUS TEST (50 POINTS)	Moderate Priority • Spelling test (10 points) • Math homework (10 points) • Soccer practice and games
No Deadline or Distant Deadline	Moderate Priority • History term paper (250 points)	Low Priority • Play Playstation / beat brothers score • Chat with friends online • Extra soccer practice

Figure 23. Example of a completed Decision Matrix for Prioritization. All items from the Goals Worksheet are evaluated and placed in the appropriate box on the Decision Matrix so that the student can begin to prioritize his goals.

Teaching this Strategy

- The student will need to go through the items on the Goals Worksheet and determine which box each item belongs in on the Decision Matrix.

- It may be necessary to have the student work through the potential outcomes of some tasks using the basic "Thinking Tool" so that he can determine the potential bonus or penalty outcomes (refer back to Figure 21).

- Have the student cross off each item on the Goals Worksheet as it is placed on the Decision Matrix.

- The order within each box on the Decision Matrix is irrelevant at this point. The student will learn to rank the items within each priority level next using the Priorities Ladder.

- The Decision Matrix may be utilized frequently as part of the daily planning process; anytime new or additional tasks or demands are made.

Creating a Priorities Ladder

Now that the student has placed a preliminary value on each item and has categorized each as high, moderate, or low, he/she should rank and sequence each item within each priority level. This can be done using the Priorities Ladder (refer to Figure 24).

Priorities Ladder

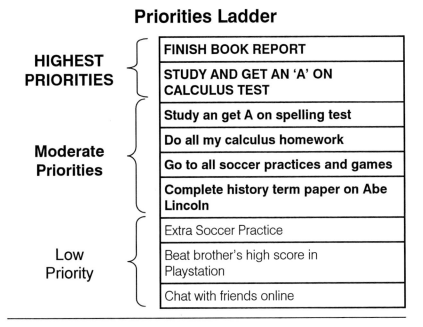

HIGHEST PRIORITIES	**FINISH BOOK REPORT**
	STUDY AND GET AN 'A' ON CALCULUS TEST
Moderate Priorities	**Study an get A on spelling test**
	Do all my calculus homework
	Go to all soccer practices and games
	Complete history term paper on Abe Lincoln
Low Priority	Extra Soccer Practice
	Beat brother's high score in Playstation
	Chat with friends online

Figure 24. Example of the Priorities Ladder Worksheet. The items from the Decision Matrix were ranked here within each priority level.

Teaching this Strategy

- Have the student look at all of the items in the high priority box on the Decision Matrix. Since all of these have high bonus or penalty outcomes, have the student rank them initially by due date, with the item having the most immediate due date going on the top rung of the Priorities Ladder.

- Have the student go through and rank the moderate priority items and then the low priority items, also placing them on the Priorities Ladder.

- The student should then have a hierarchy of goals and priorities to work from when updating the monthly calendar and the daily schedule.

- When new tasks or demands are added, they should be evaluated using the criteria from the Decision Matrix and placed in the appropriate location on the Priorities Ladder. This should be discussed each day during the designated planning routine(s).

- When the items are completed, they should be removed from the ladder, and the subsequent items should be moved up a rung.

- Essentially, the student is using a self generated, prioritized, to do list to accomplish his/her goals!

Prioritized Planning

In the previous chapter, the student was taught to fill in the monthly calendar with regularly occurring routines or events, irregular routines or events, and components of complex tasks or assignments. So far, the student has been taught to "follow" a time management procedure. He/she should be able to answer "how" questions about time management and planning. However, the student still has not been forced to apply the underlying evaluation skills and critical thinking necessary to truly become effective with prioritized planning. He/she has not yet been required to answer the "why" portion of planning and time management, which is critical for goal directed behavior. It is now time to integrate these pieces. In prioritized planning, the student follows the procedures for time management that he/she has learned, yet he/she must also begin to use his/her evaluation skills to think through the outcomes of his/her actions when "developing" and "adjusting" the daily schedule(s) and monthly calendar.

Adjusting the Monthly Calendar

Once the student has identified and ranked his/her goals and priorities for the month, as described above, he/she can complete the monthly calendar incorporating that information. When new assignments or activities are scheduled, the student will need to make the necessary accommodation in his/her monthly calendar using the strategies for prioritized planning.

Teaching this Strategy

- During the last planning session of the month, the student should fill in the next month's calendar following the procedure for completing the monthly calendar that was taught in the previous chapter .

- Each day during the planning session, any new items or items that were not completed from the previous day will need to be added to the calendar.

- If or when a scheduling conflict arises, the student will need to determine how to adjust the calendar. This can be done by utilizing the Decision Matrix and Priorities Ladder. The student needs to evaluate the competing items using the Decision Matrix and then rank them on the Priorities Ladder.

- Next he/she will need to determine which of the conflicting items is a higher priority (i.e., is higher on the Priorities Ladder) and then "bump" the lower priority.

- He/she will need to determine if and when the "bumped" item can be rescheduled. This is done by having the student look at each of the scheduled items chronologically, between the current date and that "bumped" items due date. When he/she comes to an item which ranks as a low priority (or "free time"), that item could be "bumped".

- If there are no low priority items between the current date and the "bumped" items due date, the student should do a chronological search for any item which ranks lower on the Priorities Ladder than that current "bumped" item. He/she must then bump the lower of the two and fill in the higher. This bumping process should continue until he/she is down to bumping a low priority item.

- Once the student has bumped down to a low priority item, he/she should evaluate whether or not to attempt to reschedule that item, or simply put it on the reminder board as a potential goal for the following month.

Review

To demonstrate how prioritized planning works, let's go through a scenario where the entire process is necessary. Assume our student was assigned a science project on Friday, September 18th that is due on Tuesday, September 22nd. He guesstimates (using the process he learned from Chapter 3) that the assignment will take 4 hours of work time to complete. The assignment is worth 50 points. The following review section illustrates the process the student must go through in order to accommodate this new assignment using the prioritized planning process (refer to steps 1-4, Figures 25a - 25d).

SEPTEMBER 2004						
Sunday	Monday	Tuesday	Wednesday	Thursday	Friday	Saturday
		1	2	3	4	5
		Research Lincoln 3:00 - 5:00	Research Lincoln 3:00 - 4:00 Soccer Practice 5:00 - 6:00	Study Spelling	Spelling test Free time 4:00 - 6:00	Soccer Game 12:00 - 1:00
6	7	8	9	10	11	12
Research Lincoln 3:00 - 5:00	Write out-line for Lincoln Report 4:00 - 6:00	Outline for Lincoln Due	Study Calculus Soccer Practice 5:00 - 6:00	Study Spelling Study Calculus	Spelling Test Free time 4:00 - 6:00	Soccer Game 8:00 - 9:00 Beach Trip 11:00
13	14	15	16	17	18	19
Beach Trip Study Calculus	Calculus test Work on Lincoln rough draft 5:00 - 6:00	Work on Lincoln rough draft 4:00 - 6:00	Study Spelling Soccer Practice 5:00 - 6:00	Rough draft for Lincoln Report Due Study Spelling	**Spelling Test Free time 4:00 - 6:00**	**Soccer Game 9:00 - 10:00 Soccer Picnic 1:00 - 4:00**
20	21	22	23	24	25	26
Work on Book Re-port 9:00 - 12:00 Movies 2:00 - 5:00	**Work on Book Report 4:00 - 6:00**	**Science Project Due Work on Book Re-port 4:00 - 6:00**	Study Spelling Soccer Practice 5:00 - 6:00	Book Report Due Study Spelling	Spelling Test Free time 4:00 - 6:00	Soccer Game 10:00 - 11:00
27	28	29	30			
Revisions to Lincoln Report 9:00-12:00	Prepare final Lincoln Report 5:30 - 6:00 Dr. Apt 3:30	Final Draft for Lincoln Report Due	Study Spelling Soccer Prac-tice 5:00 - 6:00			

Step 1 (Figure 25a.): The student should begin by looking at the current calendar which already includes all scheduled events (high and low priority). The dark shaded section depicts the area of the calendar that needs to be revised to accommodate the new science assignment. The student should write in the new assignment's due date (indicated here by underlined text).

	Heavy Bonus or Penalty Outcome	No or Light Bonus or Penalty Outcome
Urgent Deadline	**HIGH PRIORITY** • **SCIENCE PROJECT (50 PT)** • **BOOK REPORT (100 PT)**	**Moderate Priority** • **Soccer Game**
No Deadline or Distant Deadline	**Moderate Priority**	Low Priority • Soccer picnic • Movies • Free time

Step 2 (Figure 25b): Next, the student should complete a revised Decision Matrix for Prioritization. This includes the science project and all other scheduled activities between it's assignment date and due date, those in the darker shaded area of Figure 25a.

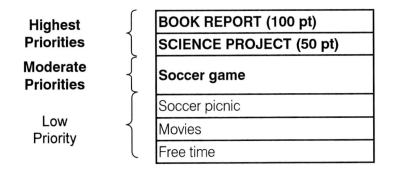

Step 3 (Figure 25c.): The student then completes a revised Priorities Ladder with all of the items from the Decision Matrix. He ranks the book report higher than the science project because it is worth more points.

SEPTEMBER 2004

Sunday	Monday	Tuesday	Wednesday	Thursday	Friday	Saturday
		1 Research Lincoln 3:00 - 5:00	**2** Research Lincoln 3:00 - 4:00 Soccer Practice 5:00 - 6:00	**3** Study Spelling	**4** Spelling test Free time 4:00 - 6:00	**5** Soccer Game 12:00 - 1:00
6 Research Lincoln 3:00 - 5:00	**7** Write outline for Lincoln Report 4:00 - 6:00	**8** Outline for Lincoln Due	**9** Study Calculus Soccer Practice 5:00 - 6:00	**10** Study Spelling Study Calculus	**11** Spelling Test Free time 4:00 - 6:00	**12** Soccer Game 8:00 - 9:00 Beach Trip 11:00
13 Beach Trip Study Calculus	**14** Calculus test Work on Lincoln rough draft 5:00 - 6:00	**15** Work on Lincoln rough draft 4:00 - 6:00	**16** Study Spelling Soccer Practice 5:00 - 6:00	**17** Rough draft for Lincoln Report Due Study Spelling	**18** **Spelling Test** <u>Work on Science Project</u> <u>4:00 - 6:00</u>	**19** **Soccer Game 9:00 - 10:00 Soccer Picnic 1:00 - 4:00**
20 **Work on Book Report 9:00 - 12:00** <u>Work on Science Project 2:00 - 5:00</u>	**21** **Work on Book Report 4:00 - 6:00**	**22** <u>Science Project Due Work</u> **on Book Report 4:00 - 6:00**	**23** Study Spelling Soccer Practice 5:00 - 6:00	**24** Book Report Due Study Spelling	**25** Spelling Test Free time 4:00 - 6:00	**26** Soccer Game 10:00 - 11:00 **Movies 1:00 - 5:00**
27 Revisions to Lincoln Report 9:00-12:00	**28** Prepare final Lincoln Report 5:30 - 6:00 Dr. Apt 3:30	**29** Final Draft for Lincoln Report Due	**30** Study Spelling Soccer Practice 5:00 - 6:00			

Step 4 (Figure 25d.): Finally, the student should revise the Monthly Calendar. He should include all scheduled work time for the high priority tasks and do the necessary "bumping" of the lower priority tasks. In this figure, the work time for the science project is indicated by the underlined text. Our student needed to "bump" his Sunday movie to schedule work time for the science project, but he was able to reschedule the movie for the following Saturday (refer to bold text).

Creating and Adjusting the Daily Schedule(s)

The daily schedules are used to help the student achieve his/her goals in a timely manner and stay on track with goal directed behavior. They help the student to transition from one activity to another, independently. The student should now have the process down for using the daily schedule(s). In addition, he/she has had many opportunities to observe and work with a parent or teacher when developing them. Now it is time for the student to take over the development of the daily schedule(s) for him/herself. As mentioned in Chapter 1, it is often helpful to create several daily schedules depicting different parts of the student's day (refer back to the examples in Figures 14a and 14b).

Teaching this Strategy

- Each day, the student should look at the monthly calendar and create the daily schedule(s) based on the items plotted out on the calendar for that day.

- If there were items on the calendar from the previous day that were not completed or if new items/demands have been added, the student will need to re-prioritize and adjust the monthly calendar accordingly prior to making that days schedule, using the same process described above.

- Once the items have been ranked, the student can evaluate that day's schedule and determine which item(s), if any, need to be "bumped" and rescheduled on another day in the month. He/she should revise the rest of the monthly calendar accordingly (i.e., evaluating and plugging in any bumped items into other days in that month).

- The student should fill out a daily schedule checklist, as described in the previous chapters, to assist him/her with maintaining goal directed behavior throughout the day.

- If the student is using a PDA, programming the alarm or time can be very helpful in assisting the student in staying on schedule.

Prioritization Skills and Goal Directed Behavior: Structure

Structure includes modifications to the materials, environment, or routines that will better accommodate the needs of a person. In Chapter 2, the importance of establishing planning routines at home and at school was discussed. It is imperative to be consistent with these planning routines! It is during these routines that priorities are evaluated and goals are set. If these routines are not carried out consistently, with support from parents and teacher, the student may become frustrated with the entire R.O.P.E.S. process.

Bright Idea

If there are times when two high priority tasks directly compete with each other, and there is no way the student will be able to complete them both (even when all other lower priority items are bumped), the determination of which item to eliminate will need to be based on the bonus or penalty value and the long-term outcome of not completing each task. For example, if a book report and the calculus test are both worth 100 points and are due on the same day, the one with the smaller long-term negative outcome should be bumped. If the student has a much lower grade in Literature (currently a C-) than in calculus (currently an A-), the long-term penalty outcome of not doing the book report is much more severe than that of not studying for the calculus test. So, if he/she must eliminate one or the other, the study time for calculus must be eliminated. These long-term outcomes can be evaluated using the basic "Thinking Tool."

If the student is constantly operating in this kind of crisis mode (i.e., there are always many high priority items that are competing), the expectations of the student should be reevaluated. Perhaps he/she has a school schedule that is too demanding or perhaps he has too many extracurricular activities. Keep in mind that this entire process of planning, organizing and prioritizing will take a substantial amount of time initially, so make the necessary accommodations for extra time.

Prioritization Skills and Goal Directed Behavior: Supports

Supports are any type of assistance from others or specific devices that will help facilitate independence. So, if we review the above recommendations, this will include:

- Basic "Thinking Tool" Worksheet
- Goals Worksheet
- Decision Matrix for Prioritization
- Priorities Ladder
- Time management systems (calendars and schedules).
- Committed teachers and parents who will be consistent and use good behavioral teaching strategies while the student learns the R.O.P.E.S.

Chapter 4

Evaluation and Critical Thinking Skills

Understanding Evaluation and Critical Thinking Skill Deficits in Individuals with High Functioning Autism

As discussed in the previous chapter, students with high functioning autism often do not see the relationship of their actions to the outcomes that ensue. Further, due to deficits in their ability to see similarities and make comparisons, they are not able to utilize their learning history to make current judgments and action plans. This is why novel demands and situations are so anxiety provoking for students with executive dysfunction and autism. Most of us are able to draw on our previous experiences, which allow us to develop some ideas about expectations when in a novel situation. We use this knowledge to develop an action plan or a strategy for how to act in the new situation. Although new situations or demands may make us nervous (think of your first day on a new job), we easily overcome these feelings and rise to the challenge.

People with high functioning autism are not naturally able to access their prior learning histories in order to devise an action plan or strategy for dealing with the novel situation. They may attempt to compensate for these deficits by developing and memorizing rules. They attempt to apply a rule to everything so that they can make sense of the world and in an attempt to develop strategies for handling every situation. These rules are often called rituals or rigid patterns of thinking and behaving. They are often looked at as unchangeable characteristics of autism. However, if we teach these students a way to think through novel situations by drawing on their previous experiences and evaluating their actions and outcomes, we can provide them with life changing skills to overcome these "inappropriate" behaviors.

The Operational Definition of Evaluation and Critical Thinking Skills

The ability to predict outcomes in novel and familiar situations and then chose appropriate actions that will result in positive or desirable outcomes. This includes the ability to recognize and adjust behavior if it is not resulting in the desired outcome.

Evaluation and Critical Thinking Skills: Strategies

Strategies are those behaviors and skills that are taught to help a person overcome or compensate for his/her deficits. In the following section some strategies for helping individuals with high functioning autism to overcome and/or compensate for deficits in evaluation and critical thinking skills will be discussed.

Teaching Self-Evaluation

As has been discussed in the introduction of this chapter and in the preceding chapters, a major deficit in persons with high functioning autism and executive dysfunction is the ability to think ahead to the potential outcomes of their actions. In the last chapter we introduced the situation-action-outcome continuum using the basic "Thinking Tool" to visually represent how this sequence works. This visual model can be applied to any situation in order to help the person self-evaluate (Cafferata, G., 2002). By doing so he/she will also develop the critical thinking skills necessary to make choices and adjust his/her own behavior to obtain more desired outcomes.

Teach Self-Evaluation of Problematic Behaviors

It may be necessary to place immediate emphasis on problematic behaviors being exhibited by student if they are interfering with learning. As part of a comprehensive positive behavior intervention plan, the student must learn to look objectively at his/her own behavior. This can be done using the "Thinking Tool" as structured in the Evaluating and Resolving Problematic Behavior Worksheet (refer to Figure 26). By learning to evaluate his/her own problematic behavior, the student will begin to see the relationship between behaviors and consequences. He/she will learn, in context, about emotions, stress, and sensory needs. He/she will learn to self-manage behaviors and choose more effective actions in the future. He/she will gain valuable insight into the affect behavior has on others (perspective taking skills).

This model will provide the student with the visual structure needed to begin to evaluate his/her own problematic behaviors. By actively participating in this process, the student is helping to develop his/her own positive behavior intervention plan. He/she is giving direct input into the behavioral choices and seeing the potential outcomes of appropriate choices, thus buying into the plan. This has been an invaluable tool is developing successful behavior intervention plans with higher functioning students.

Teaching this Strategy

- Typically, when a student engages in the identified "maladaptive behavior," there is a consequence implemented in an attempt to decrease or interrupt the behavior. Once implemented, as indicated by his/her individualized behavior intervention plan, and the student has had an opportunity to deescalate, he/she should fill out the Evaluating and Resolving Problematic Behavior Worksheet. Often this can become part of the compliance check procedure specified in the behavior plan to ensure the student is emotionally ready to resume the classroom or home activity.

Evaluating and Resolving Problematic Behavior

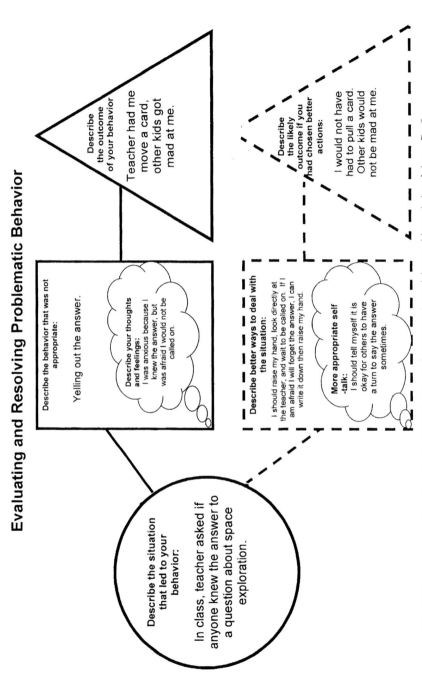

Describe the situation that led to your behavior:

In class, teacher asked if anyone knew the answer to a question about space exploration.

Describe the behavior that was not appropriate:

Yelling out the answer.

Describe your thoughts and feelings: I was anxious because I knew the answer, but was afraid I would not be called on.

Describe the outcome of your behavior

Teacher had me move a card, other kids got mad at me.

Describe better ways to deal with the situation:

I should raise my hand, look directly at the teacher, and wait to be called on. If I am afraid I will forget the answer, I can write it down then raise my hand.

More appropriate self -talk: I should tell myself it is okay for others to have a turn to say the answer sometimes.

Describe the likely outcome if you had chosen better actions:

I would not have had to pull a card. Other kids would not be mad at me.

Figure 26. Example of the **Thinking Tool** applied to evaluating and resolving problematic behaviors. By completing this worksheet, the student is participating in the development of his/her own behavior intervention plan.

- Initially the parent or teacher will need to provide a lot of prompting and positive feedback while working with the student to complete the components of the worksheet.

- Once the student understands the process, he/she should be expected to complete the worksheet independently, with feedback from staff or parent only after the entire worksheet is completed. The student may need to practice filling in the worksheet many times with someone before he/she is able to complete the worksheet independently.

- The student should practice this process for several different behaviors to promote generalization. The targeted behaviors do not need to be extreme or dangerous. They could be behaviors such as talking out in class, interrupting others, making clicking sounds, etc.

- The eventual goal is for the student to complete the worksheet independently, with eighty percent accuracy (his/her responses correspond with staff at least eighty percent of the time) and for this process to directly result in the targeted maladaptive response decreasing and the identified alternative behavior increasing.

- Eventually the student may "think" through this process prior to engaging in maladaptive behavior or to adjust his/her future behavior. If the student continues to need the worksheet to organize his/her thoughts, this is acceptable.

- Many students do begin to think through situation-action-outcome scenarios hence the reason this invaluable graphic organizer has been named the "Thinking Tool."

Creating Action Plans and Making Good Choices

This process is similar to the one described above, where the student uses the "Thinking Tool" to evaluate his/her actions and potential outcomes. However, in this format, begin working with the student on being proactive with the model. Ideally, we would like the student to inhibit his/her responses long enough to think through potential outcomes. This requires that he/she understand that there are multiple actions possible in any given situation and that potential outcomes of those actions can be reasonably predicted ahead of time. This prediction ability is very important because it is the prediction about the likely outcome that will help the student to select the most appropriate action in any given situation. This model also helps the student to become more flexible in thinking as he/she understands that there may be multiple correct or appropriate ways of responding in any given situation.

Using the "Thinking Tool" for Making Good Choices and Selecting Appropriate Actions

This variation of the "Thinking Tool" provides the visual structure necessary for the student to organize his/her thoughts and work through the potential outcomes of his/her actions so that he/she can make good choices (see Figure 27. Although the student may need to utilize this worksheet for quite some time, eventually he/she may acquire the ability to think through this process in the actual situation.

Evaluating and Selecting Appropriate Actions

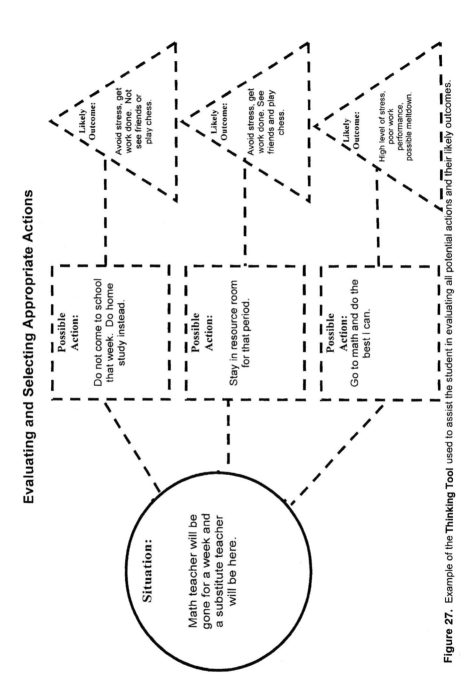

Situation:

Math teacher will be gone for a week and a substitute teacher will be here.

Possible Action:

Do not come to school that week. Do home study instead.

Likely Outcome:

Avoid stress, get work done. Not see friends or play chess.

Possible Action:

Stay in resource room for that period.

Likely Outcome:

Avoid stress, get work done. See friends and play chess.

Possible Action:

Go to math and do the best I can.

Likely Outcome:

High level of stress, poor work performance, possible meltdown.

Figure 27. Example of the **Thinking Tool** used to assist the student in evaluating all potential actions and their likely outcomes.

Teaching this Strategy

- Because we would like this to become a proactive strategy, it is best to begin utilizing this worksheet to address upcoming situations as opposed to situations that have already occurred, as we did with the Evaluating and Resolving Problematic Behavior Worksheet. The first step is to identify a situation which will soon occur that the student needs to prepare for. Once the situation is identified, the student can fill in the circle portion of the worksheet.

- Next, the student should identify a possible action plan for dealing with the identified situation. This should be written in the top square. Note: The student is usually able to come up with one action plan with minimal prompting, but will usually have a more difficult time with predicting the outcome and identifying other possible action plans. This will require prompting from a parent or teacher.

- After the initial action plan has been identified by the student, ask him/her to predict the likely outcome of that action. Have him/her write the response in the top triangle.

- Prompt the student to come up with another possible action plan for the situation. This may require very explicit prompting initially.

- Once the second action plan is identified, have the student attempt to predict the likely outcome of that action and write it in the second triangle.

- Complete the process with the third action plan and likely outcome.

- It is best to demonstrate a variety of potential action plans, some with really positive outcomes, others with fairly negative outcomes. This will help the student with the final step of this process, which is identifying the "best" action plan for the situation.

- This final step is accomplished by having the student evaluate the outcomes (triangles), then determine which is the most desirable outcome in the current situation. Have the student circle the most desirable outcome and possible action plan (square) to obtain it.

- The information contained within the square can then be expanded and developed into the action plan. This action plan can then be broken down into a checklist, as described in the previous chapters. If there are multiple components to recall; or it can be put on an Action Plan Card as described in the coming section to remind the student of what to do.

Using Action Plan Cards

Once the student has identified an action plan for a certain situation, visual cues can be used to help him/her recall the plan. It is a good idea to utilize these visual cues as part of a positive behavior support plan when the student is developing the necessary alternative behaviors. For example, if the problematic behavior was calling out answers in class and the more appropriate alternative is to write the answer down, raise a hand, and wait to be called on, the Action Plan Card could be used to remind the student of the appropriate response to use (see Figure 28).

Action Plan Card

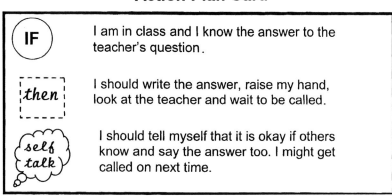

Figure 28. Example of an Action Plan Card developed for recalling appropriate actions in a given situation. This card would be placed on the student's desk or some other location to cue him/her to choose the appropriate action.

Teaching this Strategy

- Start by having the student complete the Action Plan Card based on the action identified from the Evaluating and Selecting Appropriate Actions Worksheet.

- Have the student identify a location(s) to keep the card that will cue him/her in the relevant situation(s).

- Post the card in all of the identified locations.

  If the student utilizes the strategy as specified on the Action Plan Card, provide a reinforcer. This may be some type of identified reinforcer such as tokens, points or a tangible reward.

- If the student does not use the strategy specified on the Action Plan Card in the relevant situation, the teacher or parent should prompt him/her by simply pointing to or tapping the card. Once the student utilizes the strategy, reward with verbal praise only. No tangible or token reward is given for prompted responses.

- The Action Plan Card will eventually cue the student to stop and think about what he/she should do prior to engaging in the problematic behavior. The card can also be used as part of a comprehensive self monitoring plan as described in the final chapter.

Evaluating Novel Situations

As was discussed in the introduction, people with autism are not equipped to deal with novel situations until they learn to make the connection with previous experiences and then draw on those experiences. In Chapter 2, the Venn diagram was used to compare and contrast novel tasks and previously experienced tasks when teaching "guesstimation." In Chapter 3 the "Thinking Tool" was introduced. To effectively evaluate novel situations and draw on previous experiences, a combination of these graphic organizers is utilized.

Using the "Thinking Tool" Model for Evaluating Novel Situations

This model helps to prepare the student for dealing with novel situations by showing him/her how to select behaviors and predict potential outcomes based on similar situations he/she has encountered in the past. It shows him/her how to draw on past experiences when encountering novel situations. This skill can help the student to overcome

Evaluating Novel Situations

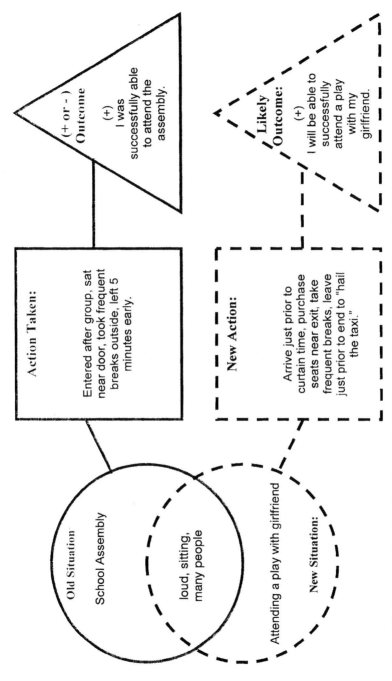

Figure 29. Example of the **Thinking Tool** applied to the evaluation of novel situations and experiences. This combination of the **Thinking Tool** and Venn diagram allow the student to draw on previous, similar experiences to develop an action plan for dealing with the novel situation.

(+ or –) Outcome

(+)
I was successfully able to attend the assembly.

Likely Outcome:

(+)
I will be able to successfully attend a play with my girlfriend.

Action Taken:

Entered after group, sat near door, took frequent breaks outside, left 5 minutes early.

New Action:

Arrive just prior to curtain time, purchase seats near exit, take frequent breaks, leave just prior to end to "hail the taxi."

Old Situation

School Assembly

loud, sitting, many people

Attending a play with girlfriend

New Situation:

problems with rigidity/inflexibility that often result when he/she is faced with novel challenges. The model is best utilized in context (i.e., when the student is encountering the new situation) or in advance of an upcoming novel event to teach the student to think through the novel situation without having behavioral problems or reverting to some rigid pattern of behavior.

Teaching this Strategy

- Begin by having the student identify the novel situation and write it on the Evaluating Novel Situations Worksheet in the dashed circle as shown in Figure 29.

- Next, assist the student in identifying an old situation or a previously experienced situation that is similar, much like he/she did in Chapter 2, when learning to guesstimate.

- Once a similar situation is identified, have the student compare it to the new situation utilizing the Venn diagram portion of the worksheet. He/she will identify the similarities and write them where the solid circle and dashed circle overlap and then the differences, which he/she will write in the appropriate circles.

- Next the student should look at the previous experience and write in the action that was taken (in the solid square), and the outcome that resulted (in the solid triangle).

- He/she should indicate whether the outcome was desirable (+) or undesirable (-) in that situation.

- If the outcome from the previous action plan was positive (+), the student should adopt that action plan or a similar one for the current situation.

- If the outcome of the previous action plan was negative (-), he/she should adopt a different action plan. This may require working through the critical thinking skills model for Evaluating and Selecting Appropriate Actions as described on pages 142 - 144.

Evaluation and Critical Thinking Skills: Structure

Remember that structure includes modifications to the materials, environment, or routines that will better accommodate the needs of a person. In this section evaluation and critical thinking skills were discussed including ways for individuals with autism to determine and predict the outcomes of their behavior. The structure they need to apply these new strategies involves visual reminders.

Post Action Plan Cards

Place Action Plan Cards where the student can see them. The visual will cue the student to choose the pre-determined action plan that will result in the desirable outcome.

Evaluation and Critical Thinking Skills: Supports

Supports, again, are any type of assistance from others or specific devices that will help facilitate independence. So if we review the recommendations from above this will include:

- "Thinking Tools"
- Action Plan Cards
- Committed teachers and parents who will use good behavioral teaching strategies while the student learns the R.O.P.E.S.

Chapter 5

Self-Management

Understanding Self-Management Deficits in Individuals with High Functioning Autism

People with high functioning autism are often eager to learn new skills; however, they may also become very dependent on others to assist them in generalizing these skills and in using the skills functionally. They often become dependent on others for cuing, feedback and reinforcement, even when they have learned the steps for task completion. Although the initial learning of many of the target behaviors discussed so far is critical, if the student is not able to self-manage, he/she will continue to rely heavily on others and will likely never become self-sufficient.

Self-management is a technique that facilitates inde-pendence by systematically fading reliance on external controls (e.g., praise, feedback, and instructions) and shifting control to the child (Smith, L., and Fowler, S., 1984). Cooper, Heron and Heward define self-management as "the personal and systematic application of behavior change strategies that result in the desired modification of one's own behavior" (Cooper, J., Heron, T., and Heward, W., 1987). Research has shown that when self-management of specific target behaviors is taught there is also a significant decrease

in other maladaptive behaviors that have not been specifically targeted for intervention (Koegel, L., Koegel, R., Hurley,
C., and Frea, W., 1992). In addition, research has shown that
changes in behaviors achieved through self-management
training are maintained over periods of time and across instructional settings, including settings in which there are no
trained service providers (Gardner, W., Berry, D., Cole, C.,
and Nowinski, J., 1983). Because self-management training
can produce measurable behavior changes across a variety
of behaviors not targeted for intervention, it has been identified as a critical "Pivotal Response" to teach children with
autism (Koegel, R., and Koegel, L., 1995).

One can see how addressing issues of self-
management can have life long implications for students
with autism and executive dysfunction. Teaching self-
management will decrease the need for ongoing support
and assistance that can limit a person's ability to become
self-sufficient. Not only does this type of intervention benefit
the student, it also allows parents and educational staff to
focus their efforts elsewhere and it is a cost effective use of
resources. In this chapter, strategies for increasing
self-management across many of the behaviors and skills
addressed so far in this manual will be covered.

The Operational Definition of Self-Management

The ability to identify, measure, and reinforce ones own behavior without ongoing feedback or input from other people.

Self-Management: Strategies

Strategies are those behaviors and skills that are taught to help the person overcome or compensate for deficits. In the following section some strategies for helping individuals with high functioning autism overcome and/or compensate for deficits in self-management will be discussed.

Self-Management Through Stimulus Control

By teaching the student a process for self-management, you can successfully teach him/her to be independent with almost any learned skill. There are multiple components to this self-management process. One important aspect of self-management involves stimulus control. Stimulus elements of self-management include altering the environment to cue the occurrence of certain desirable behaviors. For example, leaving the treadmill out in the living-room might prompt someone to use it more. In addition, the removal or restriction of certain things in the environment that often result in undesirable behavior is part of this stimulus control process. For example, getting rid of or removing all sweets from the house might control over-consumption of them. This manual has provided many strategies for altering stimulus elements and therefore self-management in the "Structures" segments of the previous chapters. These procedures will be expanded on in later segments of this chapter. More specific strategies for teaching self-management of stress and frustration, efficiency, and initiation, all of which involve many stimulus control factors, will be provided.

Self-Monitoring

Another element of self-management involves self-monitoring of the target behaviors. Self-monitoring, also referred to as self-recording, self-observation, self-assessment, involves the individual observing and recording the occurrence or non-occurrence of his own behavior. This is a useful tool for teaching self-management because it is necessary for a person to accurately measure his/her own behavior in order to determine if that behavior is changing in the desired direction. In addition, research has shown that the mere act of recording or monitoring ones own behavior has the effect of changing that behavior in the desirable direction (see, for example, Broden, M., Hall, R., and Mitts, B., 1971). Many self-monitoring procedures have already been introduced in the previous chapters of this manual. For example, the Time Journal and all of the "Thinking Tools" worksheets involve self-monitoring. Another method of self monitoring involves frequency recording as indicated in Figure 30.

Student's Self-Monitoring Chart

Behavior: Calling out in class (saying the answer without raising hand and waiting to be called on by teacher)					
	Mon	Tue	Wed	Thu	Fri
Interval 8:30 - 9:30	IIII	III	III	II	II
Interval 9:30 - 10:30	III	III	II	I	
Interval 11:30 - 11:30	I	I	I	I	I
Interval 11:30 - 12:30	IIII	II	I		
Interval 12:30 - 1:30					
Interval 1:30 - 2:30	I	I			
Interval 2:30 - 3:30	I		I	I	I
Totals	14	10	8	5	4

Instructor's Monitoring Chart

Behavior: Calling out in class (saying the answer without raising hand and waiting to be called on by teacher)					
	Mon	Tue	Wed	Thu	Fri
Interval 8:30 - 9:30	IIII	III	III	III	II
Interval 9:30 - 10:30	IIII	III	II	II	
Interval 11:30 - 11:30	II	I	I	I	I
Interval 11:30 - 12:30	IIII	II	I		
Interval 12:30 - 1:30					
Interval 1:30 - 2:30	II	I		I	
Interval 2:30 - 3:30	I		I	I	I
Totals	17	10	8	8	5

Reliability Check Procedure: Compare data each Friday during end of day routine.

Reliability Calculations:

Intervals in Agreement = 28

Intervals in Disagreement = 7

$$Reliability = \frac{28}{(28+7)} \times 100 = 80\%$$

Figure 30. Example of self-monitoring data form which includes the definition of the behavior being monitored and the procedure for conduction reliability checks. Shaded areas note intervals of disagreement.

Teaching this Strategy

- First, a target behavior is identified for change. The target behavior should be defined very specifically. Rather than saying, "Improve hygiene," it is better to say, "Complete all steps of a written hygiene routine or checklist." This way there is no room for interpretation or negotiation when it comes to evaluation.

- A strategy for measuring the behavior should be determined. This may include the use of special devices, such as clickers or timers, as well as some sort of data recording form (as shown in Figure 30).

- The process for measuring should be very clearly defined for the student and written out so that there is no room for negotiation. It often helps to identify what an "occurrence" is and what a "non-occurrence" is.

- Next the process for determining reliability of self-monitoring can begin. "Reliability checks" for self-monitoring can be accomplished by having the student self-monitor his/her behavior for a specified period of time, while a teacher or another assistant also measures the target behavior. At the end of the period the student and teacher will check the data to determine inter-observer agreement.

- Initially the child's accuracy in self-monitoring should be heavily rewarded with positive feedback and possibly some additional tangible rewards.

- Reliability of self-monitoring is said to be established when there is eighty percent or better inter-observer agreement for three consecutive measurement sessions (Barlow, D., and Hersen, M., 1976).

> **Remember:**
> Reliability for self monitoring will typically be determined by inter-observer agreement between the student and a designated instructor/care provider. Once the data is collected by both parties the percentages of inter-observer agreement can be determined as follows:
>
> $$\frac{\text{Agreements}}{\text{Agreements} + \text{Disagreements}} \times 100 = \underline{\quad} \text{ Percent of Agreements}$$

Self-Administering of Consequences

This is the final key component of a comprehensive self-management program. Having the person identify and self-administer his/her own reinforcers (and/or punishers) can have profound effects on behavior (for a summary of research see Cooper, J., Heron, T., and Heward, L., 1987). Part of this process for students with autism is getting them to recognize the naturally occurring consequences of their actions. The ability to evaluate the outcomes of behavior, discussed in the previous chapter, is certainly critical in this process. Without the ability to evaluate the natural outcome of their actions (i.e., use the "Thinking Tool"), they would likely not succeed with any self-management protocol. In this section, the student will learn to identify and determine delivery of additional reinforcers (for achieving his/her behavioral change goals), and additional consequences (for failure to meet the behavioral change goals). This can be done using the "Thinking Tool" for Evaluating and Determining Outcomes as illustrated in Figure 31.

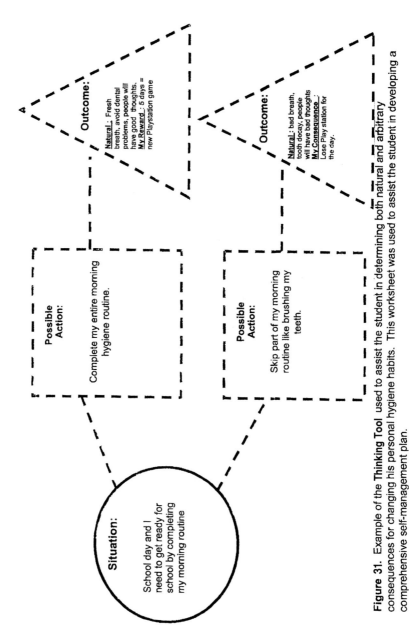

Evaluating and Determining Outcomes

Situation: School day and I need to get ready for school by completing my morning routine

Possible Action: Complete my entire morning hygiene routine.

Outcome:
Natural: Fresh breath, avoid dental problems, people will have good thoughts. My Reward: 5 days = new Playstation game

Possible Action: Skip part of my morning routine like brushing my teeth.

Outcome:
Natural: bad breath, tooth decay, people will have bad thoughts. My Consequence: Lose Play station for the day.

Figure 31. Example of the **Thinking Tool** used to assist the student in determining both natural and arbitrary consequences for changing his personal hygiene habits. This worksheet was used to assist the student in developing a comprehensive self-management plan.

Teaching this Strategy

- Students' motivations for changing any behavior are critical to the success of a self-management program. Begin by helping the student to identify the natural consequences that may be a result of the behavior change. These could be naturally occurring positive and/or negative outcomes. For example, regular tooth-brushing will keep your teeth healthy, avoid painful dental problems and procedures, your breath fresher, and people will want to be around you more. Failure to complete regular tooth-brushing may result in tooth decay, bad breath, and people may avoid you. The student should write the naturally occurring consequences on the triangle portions of the "Thinking Tool" for Evaluating and Determining Outcomes Worksheet (refer to Figure 31).

- Next, an additional arbitrary type of positive reinforcer can be identified. This should be a reward that the student helps to select and that has been shown to be effective at increasing the future likelihood of that student's behavior in the past (Koegel, L., and Koegel, R., 1995). These arbitrary rewards should then be written on the worksheet.

  NOTE: If arbitrary or additional reward contingencies are required, they will eventually be decreased as the naturally occurring rewards begin to help the student maintain the behavior. The identified reward might then be utilized in a new self-management plan as the student moves on to another target behavior.

- Some form of "response cost" consequence can also be identified and written into the worksheet. This typically means that the student will have to forfeit or delay some type of potential reward if he/she fails to meet the criteria for behavior change. For example, if the student does not complete his morning hygiene routine as determined in his self-management plan, he/she might have to forfeit his Nintendo time that day.

Developing Written Self-Management Plans

Now that all of the necessary components of an effective self-management plan have been identified, the only thing left to do is provide the student with a visual format and teach him/her how to independently complete his/her own written self-management plan.

Remember:

Self administrating of arbitrary consequences can have significant effects when included in a self management program, however, they are not always needed to produce behavior change. Cooper, et. al., states that "Sometimes self management plans are completely effective with just stimulus control, (i.e., the recommended structural accommodation in this manual) and self monitoring strategies" (Cooper, J., Heron, T. and Heward, W., 1987). If you are seeing significant positive behavior changes following the self-monitoring procedure, it may not be necessary to include any arbitrary rewards or response cost consequences in the self-management plan. I would still advise that the student go through the critical skills model to determine natural consequences.

Using a Self-Improvement Contract

To facilitate the development and implementation of self-management plans, it is helpful to utilize the Self-Improvement Contract. This contract can be used to work on decreasing problematic behaviors, such as calling out in class (refer to Figure 32 a) as well as improving other skills and behaviors, such as completing a morning hygiene routine (refer to Figure 32 b).

Teaching this Strategy

- Introduce the Self-Improvement Contract to the student and explain that it is a tool used to allow the student to manage his/her own behaviors.

- Initially a parent or teacher may need to assist the student in completing the contract. However, the student should begin to fill out the contract independently with decreasing feedback from others and, eventually, with total independence.

- Accomplished utilizing the protocol in the previous section, Self-Administering of Consequences. Once he/she has identified the rationale for changing the behavior, he/she can write it on the contract. This may include both natural and arbitrary outcomes.

- A measurable goal should be determined and written on the contract. This is essentially the criterion for earning the reinforcer. It is usually best to set the criterion level for no more than fifty percent of the baseline, initially.

Self-Improvement Contract

 The Behavior I want to change is:
Calling out in class.

 The reason I want to change the behavior is:
It annoys people, I lose school privileges, I want to earn a new Playstation game.

 My measurable goal for the behavior is:
To decrease calling out in class to no more than 15 times per week.

 If I meet the goal then:
People will be less annoyed with me, I will keep my school privileges, I will earn a new Playstation game

 If I do not meet the goal then:
People will continue to be highly annoyed with me, I will lose my school privileges, I will not earn a new Playstation game and I will have to surrender my Playstation to Mom for one week.

 I will enlist the help of:
Ms. Baker, an action plan card and a self-monitoring chart.

 This person/device will help me by doing the following:
Ms. Baker will check the accuracy of my self moni-toring, the Action Plan Card will remind me to raise my hand and wait to be called on, the self-monitoring chart is where I will record my behavior.

Figure 32a. Example of a Self Improvement Contract to assist the student in decreasing his chosen problematic behavior "Calling out in class."

Self-Improvement Contract

 The Behavior I want to change is:
Completing all of the steps of my morning hygiene routine, consistently.

 The reason I want to change the behavior is:
So people will have good thoughs of me, so I don't have to get fillings in my teeth, so that I can earn a new Plastation game.

 My measurable goal for the behavior is:
To independently complete all of the steps of my morning hygiene routine for three weeks.

 If I meet the goal then:
People will have good thoughts about me, I might have to have fillings or a root canal, I will not get a new Playstation.

 If I do not meet the goal then:
People will have bad thoughts of me, I might have to have fillings or a root canal, I will not get a new Playstation.

 I will enlist the help of:
My morning hygiene checklist, a self-monitoring chart, and Mom.

 This person/device will help me by doing the following:
My checklist will help me remember all of the steps, the self-monitoring chart is where I will make sure that I am recording the data accurately.

Figure 32b. Example of a Self-Improvement Contract developed to assist the student in improving his chosen behavior "Completing the steps in his morning hygiene routine."

The baseline can be established using the self-monitoring procedure described earlier in this chapter.

- As indicated on the Self-Improvement Contract, the student must first identify the target behavior. This can be a behavior he/she would like to improve or increase, such as completing a hygiene routine, or a behavior he/she would like to decrease, such as calling out in class.

- The next thing the student must do is assess his/her own motivation for changing the behavior. This step is The criterion should be systematically changed as improvement is shown. For example, if the goal is for the student to independently complete a morning hygiene routine and the baseline was only two days out of five, the initial goal might be three days out of five. If the goal was to decrease talking out while increasing hand raising and the baseline was five times per hour talking out and one time per hour hand-raising, a good criterion to start with might be three times per hour or less for talking out and two times per hour or more for hand raising.

NOTE: The criterion for behavior change should be adjusted according to the student's success. If the student is successfully reaching criterion levels for a few days, then increase the expectations. If the student is not meeting criterion, it may be necessary to either decrease the expectation, reassess the reinforcers, or make sure that the student fully understands and knows how to do the identified behavior (e.g., make sure he knows how to complete all of the steps of the morning hygiene routine).

- Once the criterion is set, then a process for measuring the behavior should be specified. This might include how and with what materials the student will measure the behavior. It should also indicate how or if another person will assist with reliability checks. These pieces of the plan should be specified on the contract.

- Finally, a review and evaluation process needs to be determined. This should be indicated on the Self-Improvement Contract.

- For independent self-management, the student should be responsible for measuring the behavior without requiring ongoing reliability checks and initiating the reinforcer, if arbitrary rewards are necessary. For example, if the student meets criterion for the predetermined number of days, he would then go to the teacher or another designated person to show the data and ask for the reward.

- Eventually the student will self-administer the reward once the criterion level is met. To do this, the reward should be accessible to the student without requiring an adult to get it. Periodic data checks should take place to insure that the student is continuing to accurately keep track of the target behavior.

Bright Idea
The two most important predictors of a student's ability to successfully carry out a self-management plan are:
1. How motivated the student is to change the target behavior.
2. How much success he/she has had with previous self-management plans.
So, in order to set the student up for successful self management, make sure to initially work on behaviors he/she is very motivated to change and do everything possible can to insure success on those first few self-management plans!

Self-Management of Stress and Frustration

Initially the student will need to work on simply identifying feelings of frustration and/or stress. There are several programs in *Navigating the Social World* (McAfee, J., 2002), which specifically address identifying and coping with feelings. Once the student is successfully able to identify feelings of frustration and stress, he/she can work on strategies for evaluating and self-managing them. This can be done using the "Thinking Tool" called Self-Evaluation of Stress Triggers Worksheet (refer to Figure 33.)

Teaching this Strategy

- The student will need to identify all of the situations that result in feelings of frustration and/or stress. He/she will also need to identify all of the current ways he/she reacts or responds to these stress triggers and the outcomes of these chosen actions. This information can be gathered and recorded on the Self-Evaluation of Stress Triggers Worksheet.

- The student will need to identify possible ways of handling the stress triggers once he/she finds him/herself in them. This might include things like social scripts, self-talk scripts, deep breathing/relaxation routines, help seeking routines, etc. The action plan for dealing with these stressors should be indicated on the worksheet.

- The student needs to determine and predict the likely outcome of learning and using these coping strategies, as opposed to his/her typical response. The predicted outcome should be recorded on the worksheet. This will show the student the long-term and natural reinforcers that these alternative responses will produce.

- The student should identify ways of preventing exposure to the stress triggers. This might include things like sitting in a certain part of the room, wearing headphones to filter out certain unpleasant sounds, etc. These pre-vention strategies should be indicated on the worksheet.

- In addition to preventing exposure, a plan for self-advocacy should be developed. In this plan, the student should learn to tell others in advance what situations are stressful for him/her and devise a proactive plan for pre-venting their occurrence and/or dealing with them when they arise. These prevention and self-advocacy plans should also be indicated on the worksheet. For example, if the student knows that working in groups creates high stress, he/she might devise a self-advocacy plan for

Self-Evaluation of Stress Triggers

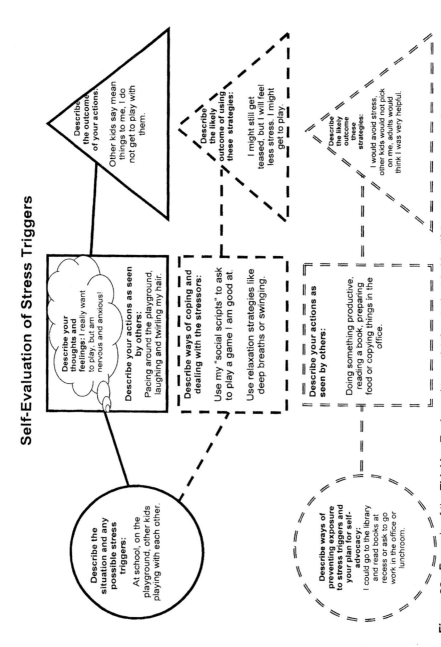

Describe the situation and any possible stress triggers:
At school, on the playground, other kids playing with each other.

Describe your thoughts and feelings: I really want to play, but am nervous and anxious!

Describe your actions as seen by others:
Pacing around the playground, laughing and twirling my hair.

Describe the outcome of your actions.
Other kids say mean things to me, I do not get to play with them.

Describe ways of coping and dealing with the stressors:
Use my "social scripts" to ask to play a game I am good at.
Use relaxation strategies like deep breaths or swinging.

Describe your actions as seen by others:
Doing something productive, reading a book, preparing food or copying things in the office.

Describe the likely outcome of using these strategies:
I might still get teased, but I will feel less stress. I might get to play.

Describe ways of preventing exposure to stress triggers and your plan for self-advocacy:
I could go to the library and read books at recess or ask to go work in the office or lunchroom.

Describe the likely outcome of using these strategies:
I would avoid stress, other kids would not pick on me, adults would think I was very helpful.

Figure 33. Example of the **Thinking Tool** used to assist the student in identifying stress triggers and developing a self-management plan and plan for self-advocacy.

telling new teachers about his/her need to work independently whenever possible.

- Once the self-evaluation and planning process described above is complete, the student could develop
and begin implementing a self-management plan for the
identified stress prevention and coping strategies using
the Self Improvement Contract previously described.

Self-Management of Efficiency

Efficiency is the ability to evaluate and self-manage
the rate of task completion. As discussed in Chapter 3, most
people with high functioning autism are not good at estimating the amount of time certain tasks will take to complete.
This is, in part, due to attention problems and staying on
task. Many times the person gets distracted from the task at
hand and, therefore, it takes them much longer than they had
expected to complete the task. Teaching these students to
evaluate and self-manage their efficiency can result in significant increases in the rate of task completion. We have already
taken one very important step in increasing or changing efficiency. We have had the student self-monitor using the Time
Journal discussed in Chapter 3. The next step is teaching
him/her how to evaluate the rate of task completion and
problem-solve how to improve and then finally self-manage it.
This can be done using the "Thinking Tool" as structured in
the Self-Evaluation of Efficiency Worksheet.

Teaching this Strategy

- Have the student identify those tasks from the Time Journal that are taking longer than expected or longer than he/she would like.

- Have the student identify any competing behaviors and distractions that are in the environment while he/she is trying to complete these specific tasks (e.g., what was he/she doing or attending to instead of the task at hand). This should be written on the worksheet. Refer to Figure 34.

- Have the student identify ways of preventing these distractions. Make a plan for eliminating the temptation to engage in the competing behavior and rearranging the environment so that the potential distractions are decreased or eliminated. Have the student write these on the worksheet.

- Have the student identify ways of increasing motivation to complete tasks in a more timely manner. This can include evaluating the natural outcomes of being more efficient (e.g., having more time for preferred activities or free time) and/or implementing some type of reinforcement system for increasing efficiency, if necessary. The student should write this information on the worksheet.

- Once this evaluation process is complete, the student could develop a written self-management plan for improving efficiency utilizing the Self-Improvement Contract described previously in Figures 32a and 32b.

Self-Evaluation of Efficiency

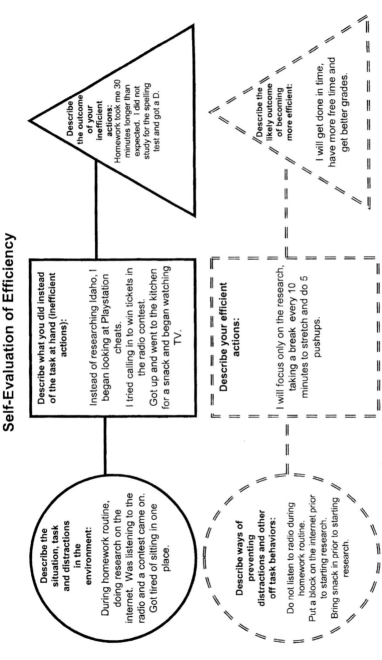

Describe the situation, task and distractions in the environment:

During homework routine, doing research on the internet. Was listening to the radio and a contest came on. Got tired of sitting in one place.

Describe what you did instead of the task at hand (inefficient actions):

Instead of researching Idaho, I began looking at Playstation cheats.
I tried calling in to win tickets in the radio contest.
Got up and went to the kitchen for a snack and began watching TV.

Describe the outcome of your inefficient actions:
Homework took me 30 minutes longer than expected. I did not study for the spelling test and got a D.

Describe ways of preventing distractions and other off task behaviors:

Do not listen to radio during homework routine.
Put a block on the internet prior to starting research.
Bring snack in prior to starting research.

Describe your efficient actions:

I will focus only on the research, taking a break every 10 minutes to stretch and do 5 pushups.

Describe the likely outcome of becoming more efficient:

I will get done in time, have more free time and get better grades.

Figure 34. Example of the **Thinking Tool** used for assisting the student at evaluating and developing an action plan to improve his/her rate of efficiency with tasks.

Self-Management of Initiation

The old saying, "You can lead a horse to water, but you can't make him drink," certainly comes to mind at this point. You have put forth a lot of effort teaching your student(s) to use all of the strategies, structures and supports outlined in the R.O.P.E.S., but will that guarantee that they will initiate the use of them when you are not there to encourage it?

According to Bromley, et al., (1995), the best way to guide the student to use graphic organizers on his/her own is to constantly model the use of them for and with the student. You may spend several months guiding your student through the process of using the R.O.P.E.S. strategies as described in earlier chapters. Once he/she is able to utilize the strategies correctly (i.e., filling out the worksheets correctly, using the calendars and checklists, etc.), the goal becomes having the student independently initiate the use of them.

As the teacher or parent, you have a three-step process to complete:

1. Acquisition (you teach the skill).
2. Transferring control to the student (you fade your cues and prompts).
3. Self-management (you conduct reliability checks).

Often times, there is a breakdown in this process, which prevents the student from achieving self-management and initiation. I have outlined many of the prompting strategies that will decrease the likelihood of "prompt dependence" as part of the procedures for teaching the skills in this manual. It is critical that the teacher does not over-prompt or make prompting errors (e.g., use direct verbal prompts rather than indirect) during the acquisition stage. In addition, the fading of your cues and prompts should be done gradually, but with purpose. The most effective teachers are those who truly understand how to select appropriate prompting strategies and fade them most effectively. If you are in need of further instruction on prompting and behaviorally based instructional strategies, The Pyramid Approach to Education In Autism (Bondy, A., and Sulzer-Azaroff, B., 2002) is an excellent resource.

The following case example illustrates how this three-step teaching process was implemented to allow this student to achieve self-management of the R.O.P.E.S.

> **Remember:**
> This is a PROCESS that we are teaching. It can take awhile for the student to become proficient at using these strategies and then in becoming independent with initiation. Once he/she gets the process down, it can have dramatic effects across many life domains (academic, social, independent living). "Students who understand how to use and create a graphic organizer have a new and valuable tool for planning, understanding, remembering, and assessing knowledge" (Bromley, K., et al., 1995).

Case Example:
Remember Alan, our very bright student who had trouble remembering his assignments and materials needed to complete the assignments? He was able to improve on these skills once he learned the R.O.P.E.S. The problem was he still required prompts from his teacher and parents to initiate the use of the system, so we set out to teach him to self manage initiation of the system as follows:

1. We taught Alan to use the homework management system with cues from teacher and parents.
2. Once he was using the systems with accuracy (fewer than three errors per week), we had him fill out the Self-Improvement Contract, specifying that he would learn to self mange the system.
3. We ran an initial phase of self-monitoring, where he could earn a reward for accuracy of self-monitoring (a new Nintendo game that his mom would buy) once inter-observe agreement was at 80 percent or better for three weeks.
4. After he was accurately self-monitoring, we started the process for self-management of his homework management system.
5. He identified all of the naturally occurring rewards for using the system independently. We then set criteria for success. Since his initial baseline was determined to be two "errors" on his homework summary page (when no prompts were provided by staff), we set criterion at no more than one error per week. This meant that he had to successfully record all assignments and materials needed with no more than one missing or incorrect pieces of information per week.
6. The criterion was systematically changed until he was able to consistently complete the log with no errors.
7. Alan was then able to self initiate the reward, turning in his completed homework log and received acceptable grades at the end of each week. Then his mom would rent him a new Nintendo game or CD of his choice.
8. Alan continued to utilize this system throughout his high school career, and from what I have heard, now in his college career (he buys himself a new computer program for passing each semester). He has learned to self-manage his bill paying and household chores in the same manner.

Alan has learned R.O.P.E.S.

Self Advocacy

As mentioned in the procedure for self-management of stress triggers, it is essential that these students learn to recognize and advocate for the things they need. A critical part of this self-advocacy process is learning about themselves and their behaviors and actions. This manual has focused heavily on teaching self-evaluation of behaviors, thoughts and actions, but there is another critical piece that students must be aware of in order to effectively self-advocate. They must learn about their disability and how it affects them.

Many parents of students with high functioning autism keep the "label" a secret from their children for fear that it will upset them or lower their self esteem. I believe that this is a mistake. These children recognize that they are different, but may not understand why. Knowledge is power, and knowledge of and about their disability will provide them with the power they need to be their own best advocates. Most children I have worked with over the years are actually relieved to finally know and understand why they experience the world differently. The book, *Asperger's ... What Does It Mean To Me?*, by Catherine Faherty, is an excellent workbook for individuals with high functioning autism to learn about the disability and how it affects them personally. The video series *Intricate Minds* by Coulter Video is another invaluable resource for self awareness.

Self-Management: Structure

Remember that structure includes modifications to the materials, environment or routines that will better accommodate the needs of a person. The structural elements that will facilitate self-management include all of those mentioned in the previous chapters and the following:

Provide a De-Stress Zone

This is a place where the student can go to de-escalate or practice relaxation techniques as determined in a plan for coping with stress triggers. Include appropriate sensory/calming activities and materials in the zone and make sure he/she knows how to do these activities. Learning these activities and how to "de-stress" may require additional interventions and supports. Working with an occupational therapist trained in sensory integration, taking yoga or ti-chi or working with a personal trainer or therapist trained in stress management and/or biofeedback are some viable options.

Self-Management: Supports

Supports, again, are any type of assistance from others or specific devices that will help facilitate independence. So, if we review the recommendations from above this will include:

- Action Plan Cards
- Self-Improvement Contracts
- Appropriate "Thinking Tools"
- Tally sheets, clickers, or other counting devices for working on self-monitoring
- Committed teachers and parents who will use good behavioral teaching strategies while the student learns the R.O.P.E.S.

References

Barlow, D., and Hersen, M., (1976). *Single case experimental designs: Strategies for studying behavior change*. New York, NY: Pergamon Press.

Baron-Cohen, S., and Swettenham, J (1997). Theory of Mind in Autsim: Its Relationship to Executive Function and Central Coherence. In D.J. Cohen and F.R. Volkmar (Eds.) *Handbook of Autism and Pervasive Developmental Disorders, 2nd Edition*. U.S.A.: John Wiley and Sons, Inc.

Bennetto, L., Pennington, B., and Rogers, S. (1996). Intact and impaired memory functions in Autism. *Child Development*, 67, 1816-1835.

Bondy, A., and, Sulzer-Azaroff, B., (2002). *The Pyramid Approach to Education in Autism*. Newark, DE: Pyramid Educational Products, Inc.

Broden, M., Hall, R., and Mitts, B., (1971). The effect of self-recording on the classroom behavior of two eighth-grade students. *Journal of Applied Behavior Analysis*, 4, 191-199.

Bromley, K., Irwin-DeVitas, L., and Modlo, M., (1995). *Graphic Organizers: Visual Strategies for Active Learning*. New York, NY: Scholastic Professional Books.

Cafferata, G. (2002). *Treating an Adolescent's Aggression: A Cognitivebehavioral Approach*. Presented at California Association of Behavior Analysis, Annual Conference, Newport Beach, CA.

Carter, C.R. (2002). *500 Ways to Organize Your Child*. Long Island, NY: Jehonadah Communications.

Cooper, J. O., Heron, T. E., and Heward, W. L., (1987). *Applied Behavior Analysis*. New York, NY: Macmillan Publishing.

Damasio A. R., and Maurer, R. G. (1978). A neurological model for childhood Autism. *Archives of Neurology*, 35, 777-786.

Dawson, G., and Lewy, A. (1989). Arousal, attention and the socioeconomic impairments of individuals with Autism. In G. Dawson (Eds.), *Autism: Nature, diagnosis and treatment* (pp.49-74). New York, NY: Guilford.

Faherty, C. (2000). *Asperger's... What Does It Mean To Me?.* Arlington, TX: Future Horizons Inc.

Fasotti, L. (2003). Executive Function Retraining. In J. Grafman and I.H. Robertson (Eds.), *Handbook of Neuropsychology, 2nd Edition.* Elsvevier Science B.V.

Flood, J., and Lapp, D. (1988). Conceptual mapping strategies for understanding information texts. *The Reading Teacher,* 41 (8), 780-783.

Frith, U. (1989). *Autism: Explaining the Enigma.* Oxford: Basil Blackwell Ltd.

Gardner, W., Berry, D., Cole, C., and Nowinski, J. (1983). Reduction in disruptive behaviors in mentally retarded adults: A self-management approach. *Behavior Modification,* 7, 76-96.

Grandin, T. (1995). *Thinking In Pictures: And Other Reports From My Life With Autism.* New York, NY: Doubleday.

Gray, C. (1994). *Comic Strip Conversations.* Arlington, TX: Future Horizons Inc.

Griffith, E., Pennington, B., Wehner, E., and Rogers, S. (1999). Executive functions in young children with Autism. *Child Development*, 70, 817-832.

Heimlich, J., and Pittleman, S. (1986). *Semantic Mapping: Classroom Applications.* Newark, DE: International Reading Association.

Hill, E.L. (2004). Executive dysfunction in Autism. *TRENDS in Cognitive Sciences,* 8, 26-32.

Hughes, C. Russell, J., and Robbins, T. (1994). Evidence for Executive Dysfunction in Autism. *Neuropsychologia*, 32, 477-492.

Keeley, S. (2003). *The Source for Executive Function Disorders.* East Moline, IL: LinguiSystems, Inc.

Kendall, P.C., and Brasswell, L., (1993). *Cognitive-Behavioral Therapy for Impulsive Children, 2nd Edition*. New York, NY: Guilford Press.

Kolberg, J., and Nadeau, K. (2002). *ADD-Friendly Ways to Organize your Life.* New York, NY: Brunner-Routledge Publishing.

Koegel, R., and Koegel, L. (1995). *Teaching Children with Autism.* Baltimore, MD: Paul H. Brookes Publishing.

Koegel, L., Koegel, R, Hurley, C., and Frea, W., (1992). Improving Social Skills and Disruptive Behavior in Children with Autism Through Self-Management. *Journal of Applied Behavior Analysis,* 25, 341-353.

McAfee, J. (2002). *Navigating the Social World: A Curriculum for Individuals with Asperger's Syndrome, High functioning autism and Related Disorders.* Arlington, TX: Future Horizons, Inc.

McEvoy, R, Rogers, S., and Pennington, B. (1993). Executive Function and Communication Deficits in Young Children with Autism. *Journal of Child Psychology and Psychiatry,* 34, No.4, 563-578.

Ozonoff S. (1995). Executive Functions in Autism. In E. Schopler and G. Mesibov (Eds.), *Learning and Cognition in Autism.* NY: Plenum Press.

Ozonoff, S. (2002). *Executive Functions in Autism.* Presented at California Association of Behavior Analysis, Annual Conference, Newport Beach, CA.

Ozonoff, S. and Griffith, E. (2000). Neuropsychological Function and the External Validity of Asperger's Syndrome. In A. Klin, F. Volkmar and S. Sparrow (Eds.), *Asperger's Syndrome.* New York, NY: Guilford Press.

Ozonoff, S., Strayer, D.L., McMahon, W.M., and Filloux, F. (1994). Executive function abilities in Autism and Tourette Syndrome: An information processing approach. *Journal of Child Psychology and Psychiatry*, 35, 1015-1032.

Pehrsson, RS., and Dehner, P.R, (1989). *Semantic Organizers: A Study Strategy for Special Needs Learners*. Rockville, MD: Aspen Publications.

Pennington, B., and Ozonoff, S. (1996). Executive functions and developmental psychopathologies. *Journal of Child Psychology and Psychiatry Annual Research Review*, 37, 51, 87.

Shallice, T., and Burgess, P. (1991). Higher cognitive impairments and frontal lobe lesions in man. In H. Levin, H. Eisenberg and A. Benton (Ed s.), *Frontal Lobe Function and Dysfunction*. Oxford: OUP.

Smith, L., and Fowler, S., (1984). Positive peer pressure: The effects of peer monitoring on children's disruptive behavior. *Journal of Applied Behavior Analysis*, 17, 213-227.

Welsh, M.E., and Pennington, B.F. (1988). Assessing frontal lobe functioning in children: Views from developmental psychology. *Developmental Neuropsychology*, 4, 199-230.

Index

Figure Index

Forms CD Index

INFORMATION HANDOUTS

SAMPLE GOALS AND OBJECTIVES

ROPES-SGO.pdf

FORMS TO PRINT AND FILL IN BY HAND

COMPANION PACK WORKSHEETS

ROPES-Forms.pdf

ROPES-01-ClusterOrganizer.pdf
ROPES-02-ClusterOrganizerRecall.pdf
ROPES-03-ClusterOrganizer02.pdf
ROPES-04-SequentialOrganizer.pdf
ROPES-05-05TaskChecklist.pdf
ROPES-05-10TaskChecklist.pdf
ROPES-05-15TaskChecklist.pdf
ROPES-06-HomeworkSummaryPage.pdf
ROPES-07-HomeworkSummaryPage.pdf
ROPES-08-MonthlyPlanningCalendar.pdf
ROPES-09-DailySchedule.pdf
ROPES-10-TimeJournal.pdf
ROPES-11-VennDiagramForComparingActivities.pdf
ROPES-12-OrganizationAndPlanningWorksheet.pdf
ROPES-13-BasicCriticalThinkingSkillsWorksheet.pdf
ROPES-14-GoalsWorksheet.pdf
ROPES-15-DecisionMatrixForPrioritization.pdf
ROPES-16-PrioritiesLadder.pdf
ROPES-17-EvaluatingAndResolvingProblematicBehavior.pdf
ROPES-18-19-BehaviorProblemSolving.pdf
ROPES-20-EvaluatingAndSelectingApproopriateActions.pdf
ROPES-21-ActionPlanCard.pdf
ROPES-22-EvaluationOfNovelSituations.pdf
ROPES-23-MonitorCharts.pdf
ROPES-24-SelfImprovementContract.pdf
ROPES-25-Self-EvaluationStressTriggers.pdf
ROPES-26-Self-EvaluationEfficiency.pdf

EXECUTIVE FUNCTIONING QUESTIONNAIRES
AND SCORING PROCEDURES

ROPES-EvaluationSet.pdf

ROPES-SelfEvaluation.pdf
ROPES-TeacherEvaluation.pdf
ROPES-ScoringProcedures.pdf

Forms CD Index Continued

FORMS TO FILL IN ON COMPUTER THEN PRINT
COMPANION PACK WORKSHEETS

ROPES-Forms-FI.pdf

ROPES-01-ClusterOrganizer-FI.pdf
ROPES-02-ClusterOrganizerRecall-FI.pdf
ROPES-03-ClusterOrganizer02-FI.pdf
ROPES-04-SequentialOrganizer-FI.pdf
ROPES-05-05TaskChecklist-FI.pdf
ROPES-05-10TaskChecklist-FI.pdf
ROPES-05-15TaskChecklist-FI.pdf
ROPES-06-HomeworkSummaryPage-FI.pdf
ROPES-07-HomeworkSummaryPage-FI.pdf
ROPES-08-MonthlyPlanningCalendar-FI.pdf
ROPES-09-DailySchedule-FI.pdf
ROPES-10-TimeJournal-FI.pdf
ROPES-11-VennDiagramForComparingActivities-FI.pdf
ROPES-12-OrganizationAndPlanningWorksheet-FI.pdf
ROPES-13-BasicCriticalThinkingSkillsWorksheet-FI.pdf
ROPES-14-GoalsWorksheet-FI.pdf
ROPES-15-DecisionMatrixForPrioritization-FI.pdf
ROPES-16-PrioritiesLadder-FI.pdf
ROPES-17-EvaluatingAndResolvingProblematicBehavior-FI.pdf
ROPES-18-19-BehaviorProblemSolving-FI.pdf
ROPES-20-EvaluatingAndSelectingApproopriateActions-FI.pdf
ROPES-21-ActionPlanCard-FI.pdf
ROPES-22-EvaluationOfNovelSituations-FI.pdf
ROPES-23-MonitorCharts-FI.pdf
ROPES-24-SelfImprovementContract-FI.pdf
ROPES-25-Self-EvaluationStressTriggers-FI.pdf
ROPES-26-Self-EvaluationEfficiency-FI.pdf

EXECUTIVE FUNCTIONING QUESTIONNAIRES AND SCORING PROCEDURES

ROPES-EvaluationSet-FI.pdf

ROPES-SelfEvaluation-FI.pdf
ROPES-TeacherEvaluation-FI.pdf
ROPES-ScoringProcedures-FI.pdf